W9-CQB-747

WEAVING

Techniques & Projects

By the Editors of Sunset Books

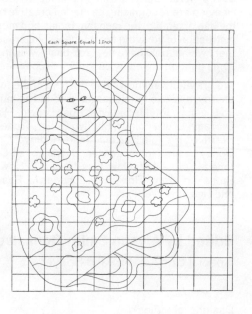

Each Square Equals 1 Inch

LANE BOOKS • MENLO PARK, CALIFORNIA

Foreword

Handcrafts in general have always been popular, but the special interest of individuals in yarn-related handwork has endured for centuries. Macramé, quilting, needlepoint, embroidery, knitting, and crocheting have in recent years enjoyed a kind of renaissance with people of all ages, in many parts of the world. And yet weaving—the one fiber art which precedes them all—has been, for the most part, a specialty of the crafts artist.

But no more. Today, growing numbers of newcomers to the fascinating world of weaving are recognizing its myriad creative possibilities. New approaches such as the use of simple, inexpensive looms and more freely structured methods in the instruction of weaving techniques, have erased much of the mystery. With this book, then, we not only have covered basic weaving techniques but have attempted to shed some light on the many delightful discoveries to be made in this idea-rich craft area.

We gratefully acknowledge the help of the following individuals whose time, talents, energy, and exciting ideas have added so much: Allied Arts Guild of Menlo Park, Ed Bigelow, Phyllis Bigelow, Russ Brown, Mary Balzer Buskirk, Paul Cleaver, Jean Darragh, Laura Folger, Marilyn Geller, Trude Guermonprez, Ed Gutowski, Kathryn Herrman, Klaudia Herrold, Sachi Honmyo, Conny Koning, John Lahr, Gyongy Laky, Docey Lewis, Nancy Lawton, Sylvia Lovell-Cooper, Lowie Museum of Anthropology, Jane Malek, Pat McGaw, Mrs. Nelson T. Nowell, Donna Oddisen, Elva Powell, Les Rhinehart, Annie Robertson, Charles M. Ross, Rose Sargeant, Pat Scarlett, and Rosalind Watkin.

Edited by Alyson Smith Gonsalves

Special Consultant: Mari Speyer

Design: John Flack

Illustrations: Marsha Kline Cooke

Cover: Quilted Tapestry Hanging (page 47), designed by Sachi Honmyo. Photographer: George Selland, Moss Photography.

Executive Editor, Sunset Books: David E. Clark

Third Printing October 1974

Copyright © Lane Magazine & Book Company, Menlo Park, Calif. First Edition 1974. World rights reserved. No part of this publication may be reproduced, by any mechanical, photographic, or electronic process, or in the form of a phonographic recording, nor may it be stored in a retrieval system, transmitted, or otherwise copied for public or private use without prior written permission from the publisher. Library of Congress No. 74- 89580. SBN Title No. 376-04751-8. Lithographed in the United States.

Contents

Unraveling the Mysteries of Weaving

LOWIE MUSEUM OF ANTHROPOLOGY, UNIVERSITY OF CALIFORNIA, BERKELEY

These two pages contain examples of some of the finest woven textiles in existence. Their intricacy, sophistication of design, and beauty of color and form reflect a high degree of inventiveness . . . yet they were created hundreds, even thousands of years ago on the most primitive of looms.

Preceded in our history only by toolmaking, weaving has been an integral part of the human pageant since the very beginning. It may have evolved from the making of twine through basketry to the discovery that plant fibers and animal fur could be twisted into strong cords and combined to make cloth. From earliest times, all woven fabric construction has been based on the system of tightly stretching a parallel series of threads (the warp) and then passing loose threads (the weft) over and under the stretched threads at right angles.

Though woven textiles dating from several thousand years B.C. can be found throughout the world, the superior weaving abilities of several civilizations have placed them in a class by themselves. The earliest examples of woven cloth may be 10,000-year-old linen fragments unearthed in Switzerland, but the most dramatic textiles have come down to us from Egypt, Peru, China, India, Africa, and the Middle East. While Egyptians were creating fine linen for use in religious garments (about 3,500 B.C.), the Chinese were guarding the mysteries of the silkworm and inventing the satin weave. In Dacca, India, around 2,000 B.C., gossamer cotton threads were being spun and woven into incredibly fine muslin gauze. At the same time, beautifully dyed, heavy woolens graced the backs of the Babylonians and formed the basis of an extensive textile trade. In all of these cultures, only the most basic of looms were used to produce fabrics.

Several centuries after the birth of Christ, Egyptian Christians, called Copts, developed a unique tapestry technique of portraiture executed in dyed wool woven onto linen threads. Coptic subjects were religious in

LOWIE MUSEUM OF ANTHROPOLOGY, UNIVERSITY OF CALIFORNIA, BERKELEY

LOWIE MUSEUM OF ANTHROPOLOGY, UNIVERSITY OF CALIFORNIA, BERKELEY

*ANCIENT EXAMPLES of weaving are a constant source of inspiration to the modern weaver. **Facing page:** Peruvian gauze and tapestry fragment dating from 1500 A.D. is also shown in color on page 74. **Far left:** Coptic tapestry strip features scenes from the life of Christ in buff, brown, blue and black wool on linen. Collected in Egypt, the piece dates from 300-400 A.D. A detail of one scene appears at lower left. **Upper left:** mummy wrapping in buff, red, yellow, and blue linens shows birds, animals, and plant motifs dating from Coptic Egypt, circa 300 A.D.*

nature, often portraits of the Disciples and Christ, or of themselves, to be used for burial ceremonies.

The Euro-Asian and African continents were not the only areas of woven textile development. Half a world away, on the shores of the Pacific in South America, was evolving one of the most impressively inventive approaches to textiles known to man. Spanning 3,500 years, craftsmen of the Inca empire slowly developed an amazing profusion of techniques and styles. Tapestry, gauze, painted cloth, pattern weaves, double cloth, ikat, brocade, featherwork, and knotted lace are just some of the techniques explored by the Peruvians. The earliest cloths, highly intricate designs based on geometrics and nature, were woven on looms that consisted of no more than two anchored horizontal sticks with warp threads stretched between them. This was later improved by the addition of a system for lifting alternating warp threads and by the use of a belt or strap at one end of the loom which passed around the back of the weaver (thus called a *back-strap loom*) and was used to control the tension of the warp threads.

Similar simple looms have been used more recently by North American Indians and various African tribes in their approaches to weaving. Stones were often used to weight the warp in the North Americas, and Africans either wove on a semi-vertical loom anchored to the ground or on small frame-like looms that produced long strips of fabric later sewn side to side.

Although there is much more to the history of weaving, including the development of textiles in Europe and colonial America, something very important is illustrated by these ancient examples. It is that the beauties of design, color, and texture in weaving depend not on the loom itself but on the individual whose tool it is. Experimentation and an adventurous spirit are the real creators of good textiles; and these "tools" may be found in anyone, anywhere.

Weaving Terms

One of the most important steps in approaching any craft is mastering the required skills. But another necessary step is that of mastering the craft's special vocabulary. This page contains a mini-glossary of weaving terms. Many of these words are discussed at greater length in the following pages, but a quick glance here will familiarize you with them ahead of time.

Beater. A comb-like or slat-like tool which is used to push the weft down into place. On floor looms, the beater consists of an attached but movable frame containing a reed.

Bubbling. One of three methods used to assure ease in the weft before it is beaten into place. The weft is passed loosely from selvage to selvage and then pushed down at 5-inch intervals before beating. This forms bubbles of warp. Other methods include arching and slanting (see page 12).

Continuous Warp. A method of warping, or preparing, a loom for weaving which utilizes one continuous length of yarn, or yarns tied end to end in a continuous length rather than a number of separate warp ends that have been consecutively measured out.

Cross. The place in a length of prepared warp where the warp ends are kept in correct order by alternatingly crossing each successive thread (see page 30).

Heading. The first few inches woven onto a new warp in plain weave before actual weaving begins. Rag strips or heavy yarn are most frequently used.

Heddle. Made from string or a flat metal strip with a centered "eye," this loom part carries and lifts each warp end to form a shed (see pages 16 and 29).

Harness. A frame or bar to which the heddles are attached. When the harness is raised, the attached heddles lift a pre-selected group of warp ends.

Pattern Weave. Any type of weave sequence based on a predetermined arrangement of warp and weft, usually as drafted out in graph form (see page 18).

Reed. A removable metal frame with vertical slots along its length, which is carried by the beater of a floor loom. Warp ends pass through these slots (called dents), keeping the ends properly spaced. The reed is also used to beat the warp into place.

Selvage. The right and left-hand edges of a woven fabric, lying parallel to the warp ends.

Sett. The density or arrangement of warp ends across the cloth. Usually refers to the number of ends per inch in the warp.

Shed. A horizontal opening made in the warp when a number of warp ends are raised. This forms a passageway for the shuttle, or weft-carrier.

Shot. One single row of weft passed through the shed. Also called pick or filling.

Shuttle. Weaving tool used to carry the weft. Shuttles range from notched sticks to boat shuttles (page 13).

Sleying. The process of threading warp ends through the dents, or openings, of the reed. Usually refers to work being done on the floor loom.

Sword. Often called the weaver's sword, this is a slat or flat stick used to create a second or extra harness, to beat down the weft, and, if pointed, to pick up selected warp ends when doing leno lace or pick-up techniques. Also called a pick-up stick.

Tapestry. A pictorial weaving technique using special methods for joining areas of color or texture to produce an overall surface design. In traditional usage, tapestry is closely allied with painting.

Threading. The portion of a pattern draft showing which harnesses will lift which warp ends, or the process of drawing warp ends through both the reed and the heddles during the warping of the loom.

Tie-Up. The portion of a pattern draft showing which harnesses are lifted together to form part of a pattern; or the act of joining together the treadles, lams, and harnesses of the floor loom in accordance with the pattern draft.

Warp. The lengthwise yarn wound onto the loom consisting of a number of individual threads each called ends. A warp-faced cloth is one in which the warp is so closely spaced that it predominated over the weft.

Weft. The yarns used to weave horizontally across the warp. Sometimes called woof or filling. Weft-faced cloth is one in which the weft is beaten down very tightly to completely cover the warp. Also see Shot.

Yarn. A continuous length of yarn, filament, synthetic or natural fiber spun for use in weaving. This is a collective term designating any material used in either the warp or the weft of a weaving.

Some Basic Theory

A marvelous analogy exists between weaving and music. The composer pens his impressions onto paper combining notes, spaces, tempo, and volume to form a musical blueprint. To the casual observer, this blueprint is just a sheet of paper covered with an arrangement of notations; yet when these notations are combined and brought forth in a performance, the whole somehow transcends each part to become a total emotional expression.

The weaver, too, may be considered a kind of composer. Using pattern, color, texture, and design, he may draft an idea out on paper as a general blueprint. When the process of weaving begins, the magic of it begins to unfold. Separate elements unite to create an entirely new and exciting impression. Pattern and design emerge, color begins to define itself, and texture becomes delightfully apparent.

Much like musical variations on a theme, a woven work may be varied. When just one element in a weaving is altered, its entire personality is transformed. There is constant excitement in weaving—of discovery, new understanding, and a growing appreciation of the flexibility of the art.

THE BASIC WEAVES

In its most basic form, weaving consists of horizontal threads alternately crossing over and under, thus interlocking with, a tightly stretched stationary field of parallel vertical threads to form cloth. The horizontal threads as a group are called weft, or filling, while the vertical threads are together known as the warp.

A seemingly endless number of ways for joining threads to make fabric exist, but they are almost all based on three basic patterns: plain weave (called "tabby"); twill weave; and satin weave. Of these three, tabby weave is the simplest, has been in existence the longest, and, because of its simplicity, lends itself most easily to a wide range of applications.

Plain weave

As illustrated in drawing 7-A, and the photo at lower right, the tabby weave is simplicity itself. The weft (or *pick*) moves across the warp, going under one warp

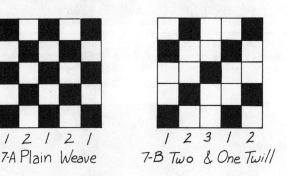

1 2 1 2 1
7-A Plain Weave

1 2 3 1 2
7-B Two & One Twill

Basic Weave Patterns

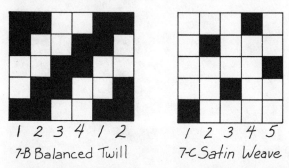

1 2 3 4 1 2
7-B Balanced Twill

1 2 3 4 5
7-C Satin Weave

GRAPHS help visually to simplify weave patterns (7-A). Black squares are warp threads on the cloth surface; white squares represent weft threads on the cloth surface.

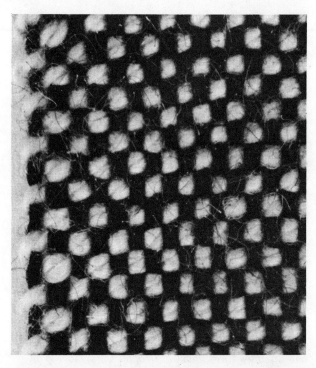

PLAIN WEAVE is the most basic of weave patterns. Also called tabby, it is formed by the alternating interlock of individual warp and weft threads as shown in drawing 7.

thread, then over the next thread, repeating this movement across the warp. At the selvage the weft returns and goes back across the warp, *over* the threads that it passed *under* in the first crossing and *under* the threads passed *over*. This locks the warp threads in place and each successive pick locks the previous pick into place. Because of its simplicity, tabby is the easiest, most economical, and most quickly made of all weaves. Though used for sheets and most printed yardage today, plain weave variations were used in the past to construct Peruvian and Coptic tapestries, Indian gauze and ikat, and Navajo blankets.

Since the technique is so basic, it may be used with ease on even the most primitive of equipment. A method for lifting alternating warp threads so that the weft can pass unhindered is all that must be added to the stretched warp. You could pick up threads by the fingers, one by one, but this soon would become tedious; so to raise all alternate threads at one time, a string is looped under each alternate thread and over a bar or stick. When all alternate threads are looped, the stick will lift them all together. After they are lifted, an opening is created (called a *shed*) for the weft to pass through. In order for the weave to lock, you must form a second shed by dropping the upper threads and raising the lower threads with another string-looped bar or a weaver's sword turned on edge. The weft may then be passed again. By alternating these sheds, you form an interlocking system, thus creating woven cloth.

Twill weave

Twill is the foundation for a vast number of pattern weaves. Characterized by distinct diagonal lines or arrangements of pattern, twill permits great variation in its appearance. Drawing 7-B and the photo at the upper right show the structure of the most elementary twill weave. Whereas plain weave requires only four threads (two vertical, two horizontal) to create its basic unit, twill needs at least six (three vertical and three horizontal). The first vertical thread is lifted and the first weft shot passes under thread one and over threads two and three. The second vertical thread is lifted and the second weft shot passes over thread three, under thread two, and over thread one. Finally, the third vertical thread rises, the weft shot passes over threads one and two and under thread three to complete the unit. (Note: Every other repeat of this series is begun at the *opposite* selvage from the starting point of the previous repeat so the first thread to be raised is *not* the first thread at the selvage, but the threads marked 1 *below the graph.)*

Twill diagonals can move from left to right or from right to left and are changed in appearance by the color, weight, and spacing of the warp and weft. Since stronger colors and heavier yarns tend to dominate when they are used in the weft and packed closely together, they form small *horizontal* bars moving in a diagonal line. This is called *weft-face twill*. Conversely, if the warp threads are dominant, small *vertical* bars form the diagonal line creating a *warp-face* twill. The

spacing of the warp and weft will also affect the slant of the diagonal twill lines.

Twill patterned fabrics have a softness, bias stretch, and drapeability that makes them a natural choice for tailored and constructed clothing or anything else requiring a pliant fabric. Plain weave, by contrast, has a rather stiff, unyielding feel and is used for upholstery, rugs, and other items in which strength and a relatively smooth surface are important.

Satin weave

Of the three basic weaves, satin is the most complex. In order for the weft threads to predominate, giving

WEFT-FACE twill **(top)** *results from horizontal bars of weft showing on the fabric surface. Warp-face twill* **(bottom)** *shows vertical bars of warp on the surface of the fabric.*

SATIN WEAVE **(above)** *derives its smooth appearance from weft threads closely packed down over warp threads that rise to the surface widely spaced from one another.*

satin its characteristic gloss and pliability, the least emphasis possible is given to the warp. Ideally, the warp threads are brought to the surface of the cloth as far apart from one another as possible. When the long floating weft threads are passed through the shed and packed, or beaten down, they tend to hide the warp threads.

As has been shown, tabby weave requires four threads and twill uses six threads for its basic unit. Satin requires a minimum of ten threads (five vertical and five horizontal). The vertical threads are raised in an order which keeps them at least one warp thread apart, as shown in drawing 7-C and the photo at lower right, page 8. The *first* vertical thread rises, and the first weft shot passes under thread one and over threads two, three, four, and five. The *third* vertical thread rises and the second weft shot passes over five and four, under three, and over two and one. The *fifth* vertical thread is raised and the third weft shot passes over threads one, two, three, and four, and under thread five. The *second* vertical thread rises, and the fourth weft shot passes over threads five, four, and three, under thread two and over thread one. Finally, to complete the unit, thread *four* is raised, and the fifth weft shot passes over threads one, two, and three, under thread four, and over thread five.

This weave is the least practical of all weaves, yet one of the most luxurious. Requiring the use of thousands of extremely fine threads to approximate satin silk as we know it, the satin weave can alternately be used in a more coarse version for very effective surface interest. An example may be seen on page 54. Because the long weft floats on the surface of the cloth, however, it is a victim of wear and snagging.

THE LOOM

Looms run the gamut from primitive stick arrangements to huge industrial power machines, but they all work on the same principles and can produce the same products with slight variations. The basic differences between them are the speed with which they turn out a finished product and the freedom of form they can adopt.

The more mechanically complex a loom becomes, the less freedom and immediate control the individual has over the weaving and its shape as it progresses. In a repetitive activity, such as making yardage, a fair amount of speed relieves the weaver of what might become a tedious job, but most woven pieces profit from the passage of time: new decisions and changes may be made; hand manipulation of the weaving and more flexibility in the final shape also become possible. Photos 9-A and 9-B at the left give a good example of the differences between floor looms and the simple backstrap looms used in Guatemala. Selvage to selvage work is quickly accomplished on the floor loom; tapestry techniques profit from the relative slowness of the backstrap.

Large, more complicated looms often restrict the weaver to a more or less rectangular shape until he or she masters an ability to overcome this restriction. This needn't be too great a concern though, for working with flexible material such as fibers and yarns allows for great variations in the type of loom used.

Branches, shaped cardboard, hoops, pin or nail boards, and a vast number of other frames can be made or converted into looms. Threads are warped onto the loom to fit its shape and are filled in with weft as desired. Often the loom becomes the frame or setting for the finished piece. Other unusually formed weavings are the result of hand manipulation, the shape of the loom becoming secondary. Pages 10 through 17 give examples and explanations of some looms that can be made and show some familiar articles that have been converted into simple weaving tools for your use.

9-A SPEED and working rhythm are two reasons that make floor looms popular among weavers of all abilities. The relative expense of this loom is its main drawback.

9-B WEAVERS in some Central American countries still work on simple looms, such as this one, not much different from those used hundreds of years ago by their ancestors.

Simple Looms

STRETCHER BAR frame looms, inexpensive and easily made, adapt well to tapestry work, plain weave, rep weave, and simple pattern weaves in a medium-sized format.

Stretcher bar frame loom. This simple loom is constructed from four canvas stretcher bars, usually sold by art supply stores. Nails are positioned along each end of the frame and yarn is wound back and forth from one end to the other to make a warp (see frame loom at far left). Weft is passed by using a tapestry bobbin or needle in the needleweaving technique (pages 20 and 21). A two-harness frame loom can be constructed from stretcher bars by making two single harness supports from plywood to hold a dowel, or harness rod. This rod carries one set of warp ends, while a flat stick inserted beneath the alternating set of threads forms a second shed when turned on its edge (see frame loom at right).

PIN AND NAIL looms can be made in just about any shape. All that's needed are pins and fibreboard or nails and some soft pine board, as well as a small hammer.

Pin and nail looms. Shaped weaving can be constructed on heavy fibreboard or soft wood boards (such as pine), using pins or nails to hold the warp, and occasionally the weft, in place. An outline of the shape to be woven is drawn on the board surface and placement of the pins is marked along this outline. Glassheaded pins are pressed into the fibreboard or nails are pounded into the soft wood at the marked points of placement, then a warp is wound onto the loom. This same procedure can be used on the edges of embroidery hoops to form circular weavings. Weft is passed with a tapestry needle or bodkin in the needleweaving technique, and looped around the nails at the end of each pass to form a finished edge.

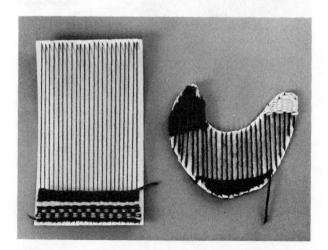

CARDBOARD LOOMS are good tools for beginners and for children. Yarn is easily wound on and worked with a needle, bodkin, or butterfly bobbin manipulated by the fingers.

Shaped cardboard looms. Heavy cardboard or illustration board can be used to make simple frame or shaped looms. A loom easily worked by children or beginners is made by cutting out a rectangle of board, marking the top and bottom edges for placement of the warp and cutting ¼-inch deep notches at these points. The warp can then be wound on the face of the loom by passing the yarn from one notched edge to the opposite notched edge, using the notches to catch and hold the turning points of the warp (see photo at near right). A shaped loom can be made in a similar manner by cutting the board in the desired shape, notching, then adding warp. Weft is passed using the needleweaving technique.

Tools and Techniques

Different looms require different methods of winding on warps and different systems for raising and lowering warp threads. The following basic approaches are those most often used and most often elaborated upon for use on other looms.

Picture frame, cardboard, and shaped looms are usually warped by winding a continuous warp thread around nails at the bottom and top or, on some frame looms, around nails at the bottom and a bar at the top (Photos 10-A, 10-B, 10-C). Floor looms and many table looms are warped from a pre-wound chain of threads treated as separate parallel entities (see pages 30-31). Four-harness frame looms are wound with a warp that passes continuously around the loom, meeting and returning at a tension rod braced in the body of the loom (see pages 16-17).

Warp threads may be lifted in different ways to form a shed, or passageway, for the weft threads.

1. One very simple method of lifting warp threads is to use a tapestry needle or bodkin to carry the weft thread. Look for more information about this technique on pages 20 and 21.

2. Two sheds may be formed by attaching every other thread with string loops to a movable harness rod that may then be lifted, and by a flat sword-like stick (called a shed stick) that is slid over these looped threads and under the alternating threads. When the stick is turned on edge, the second shed appears (see drawing 11-A).

3. The following method—a very versatile one—is used for the frame loom on page 14. It employs four harness rods instead of one. Threads are grouped and threaded onto these four rods according to a predetermined pattern. The most frequently used pattern for threading this loom, the basic 4-harness twill, is made by dividing the warp into groups of four threads. The first thread in each group is tied to harness rod 1, the

second thread in each group to harness rod 2, the third to rod 3, and the fourth to rod 4 (11-B). With this threading one can actually do two of the basic weaves: plain weave and twill.

Plain weave is created by lifting harnesses 1 and 3 together, then 2 and 4 together. Twill weave may be done in three ways: each harness—1, then 2, then 3, and then 4—lifted in succession; harnesses 1 and 2, 2 and 3, 3 and 4, 4 and 1 are lifted in succession; and harnesses 1 and 2 and 3, 2 and 3 and 4, 3 and 4 and 1, 4 and 1 and 2 are lifted in succession. The multitude of twill variations follows naturally. Pages 18 and 19 offer more information on such weaving patterns.

As you can imagine, threading the loom for four harnesses allows the weaver an enormous variety of patterns. Most floor looms used by handweavers have at least four harnesses.

WEAVING TOOLS

Shuttles, beaters, and weaving swords are a sort of supporting cast for the loom; their job is to make greater speed and precision possible. These tools may be especially designed for weaving use or converted from common everyday items. Some of the weaving equipment shown on page 13 has been adapted from such mundane purposes as combing the hair or holding an onion. So you see, tools needn't be expensive or hard to find.

Shuttles. Shuttles carry weft yarn as it is woven, keeping the yarn from tangling and moving it across the warp with more ease. They range from stick, boat, and rug shuttles to small tapestry bobbins and hand-wound butterfly bobbins (Photo 13-A, page 13). Yarn is wound onto a shuttle or bobbin, which is then passed back

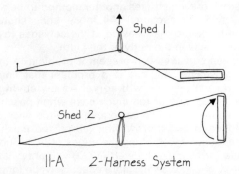

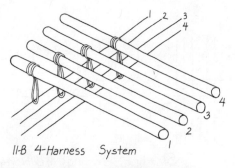

TWO WEAVING SHEDS can be easily formed by 1) a harness rod with string heddles and 2) a shed stick turned on edge **(11-A)**. Four sheds are possible on the four-harness frame loom shown on page 14 **(11-B)**. Each harness bar lifts one set of attached threads, allowing for great variety in pattern weaves and work in multiple colors.

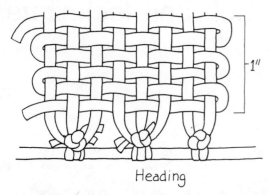

Heading

PLAIN WEAVE heading of heavy yarn or rag strips is woven for 1 inch before actual work on the project begins (12-A).

Starting the Weft

BEGIN and end any new yarn at the selvage to avoid holes or weaknesses in the middle of the woven cloth (12-B).

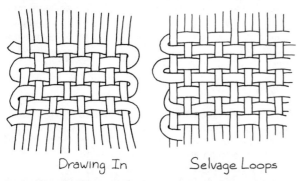

Drawing In   Selvage Loops

DRAWING IN (left) and uneven selvage loops (right) are two working problems corrected with time and practice (12-C).

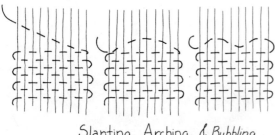

Slanting, Arching, & Bubbling

SLANTING (left), arching (center), and bubbling (right) are methods that add ease to each weft pick (12-D).

and forth through the shed from hand to hand. Throwing the shuttle, as this is called, eventually becomes an almost automatic process, and practice leads to greater speed and ease of handling. Stick and rug shuttles will hold heavier, bulky yarns; boat shuttles are used for fine yarns; and bobbins carry small amounts of yarn, specifically for tapestry or inlay work.

Beater. This tool is used to push the weft down into place (Photo 13-B). Anything from a handcarved wooden comb to a flat stick placed in the shed will work to pack weft threads at the proper density. The look and surface texture of your weaving are determined by how hard or how gently the weft is packed into place, since different weaves and techniques call for different beats. For example, tapestry and rug weaving require a very hard beat to pack the weft down tightly, covering all warp threads and giving great strength. But twill and lace weaves need room to maintain their character and therefore are formed with a light beat.

Weaver's sword. A long, flat, slightly wedge-shaped pointed stick, the sword (Photo 13-C) is used for hand-manipulated weaves and for holding open a shed. When certain warp threads are picked up by the fingers, this stick slides underneath, separating them from the unraised threads. The sword may be turned on edge to allow weft passage and then used to beat down the weft. A tool for pick-up, leno, and other lace weaves, the weaver's sword may also be called a pick-up stick.

WEAVING

The process of weaving is actually quite simple; a shed is opened, weft is passed, the shed is closed, and the weft is beaten down into place.

Before the project itself is started, about an inch of plain weave should be woven to give a firm edge to beat against (12-A). Called a heading, it also spaces the warp ends properly and sets the selvages.

On the first weft pass, leave a 1½ to 2-inch tail hanging at the selvage. Open the next shed, tuck this tail into it and then pass the second weft through the opened shed, (12-B). Use the same process when ending one thread and starting a new length or new color in designs that run from selvage to selvage (except for tapestry work which uses another method to begin and end small color sections). All loose ends should be tucked back into the weaving at the selvages to avoid any weakness in the body of the cloth.

Uneven selvages can present a problem to the beginning weaver, but this is a problem that time and growing experience will solve. As a weaving progresses, too little or too much ease when passing the weft will make uneven selvages. Too little ease draws the edges in and narrows the fabric; too much ease leaves loops of weft along the edges (12-C). Bubbling, arching, or slanting the weft (12-D) will prevent drawing in by giving the weft more ease. Selvage loops can be prevented by leaving only a small loop at the edges.

Don't worry unduly. In all cases, practice gives greater control and eventually solves these problems.

Weaving Tools

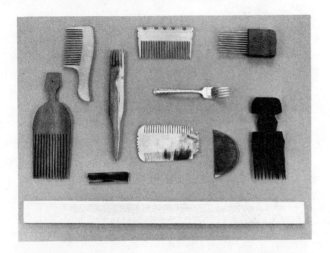

SHUTTLES (from top to bottom): butterfly bobbin, tapestry bobbin, stick shuttle, cardboard shuttle, boat shuttle, stick shuttle, rug shuttle. Each has its own specific use in weaving.

Shuttles. Used for carrying weft, shuttles are essential weaver's tools. Cardboard shuttles are easily made; stick shuttles can be purchased or cut and sanded down from a wood slat. More specialized shuttles are machined or handcrafted for weaving; these include tapestry bobbins, boat shuttles, and rug shuttles. Outside of its own shape, one weft carrier needs no physical support—that's the butterfly bobbin (page 23 shows you how to make one). These shuttles appear in the photo at the left. Other types are available, such as double bobbin boat shuttles and ski shuttles, but these are usually variations of the shuttles shown here so that a special technique can be worked.

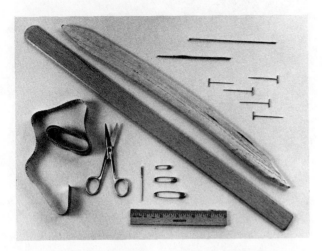

BEATERS can vary from a utilitarian table fork (center) or onion holder (upper right), to exotic hand carved African ivory and wooden combs (lower center and far right).

Beaters. Quite a few household utensils can be adapted for use in beating down the weft, such as a table fork, onion holder, hair comb, or ruler. Other tools are made specifically as beaters, including tapestry combs and stick beaters, often carved from exotic woods. Another source for beaters are handcrafted hair combs or battens from other cultures. Comb beaters with their widely spaced teeth work very well for packing down small weft areas, as in tapestry. On the other hand, when weft passes run from selvage to selvage, it requires a long, even beat; here a stick beater functions to best advantage. A variety of beaters are shown in the photo at left.

OTHER HANDY tools (clockwise from lower left): tape measure, scissors, pick-up sticks, bodkin, crochet hook, T-pins, ruler, safety pins, and tapestry needle.

Miscellaneous equipment. A few pieces of equipment are used almost constantly by the weaver, whereas others are only occasionally needed. Scissors, T-pins, a tape measure (or ruler), and safety pins are real necessities for measuring, cutting, or marking progress. Blunt-tipped tapestry needles, yarn darners, and bodkins can be used for needleweaving lace work as well as for making repairs and finishing. For leno lace work and pick-up, the weaver's sword (or pick-up stick) can come ready-made or be converted from a sanded wooden slat. As you weave, you will probably find other tools to add to this list. The weaving accessories mentioned here are shown in the photo at left.

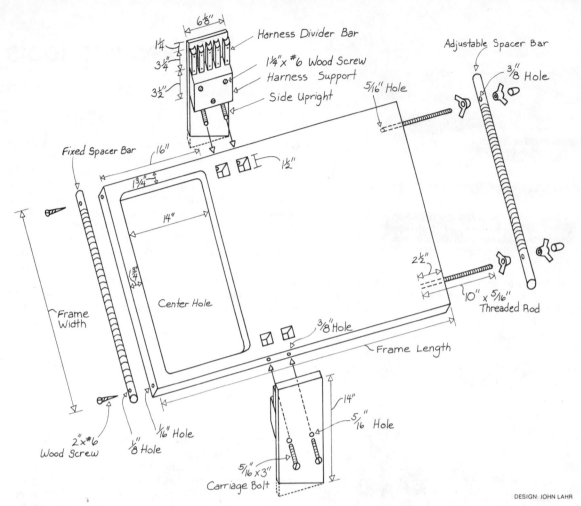

Harness Divider Bar
6⅛"
1¼
3¼"
3½"
1¼"x #6 Wood Screw
Harness Support
Side Upright
Adjustable Spacer Bar
⅜" Hole
5/16" Hole
Fixed Spacer Bar
16"
1¾"
1½"
14"
3¾"
Center Hole
Frame Width
2½"
10" x 5/16" Threaded Rod
⅜" Hole
Frame Length
14"
5/16" Hole
2"x #6 Wood Screw
1/16" Hole
⅛" Hole
5/16" x 3" Carriage Bolt

DESIGN: JOHN LAHR

MATERIALS LIST for four-harness frame loom: 3/4-inch thick plywood sheet (amount depends on loom size); six dowels (size and length depend on loom size); 35 inches of 5/8-inch half round; four 5/16-inch by 3-inch carriage bolts; two 5/16-inch threaded rods, each 10 inches long; eight 5/16-inch wing nuts; four 5/16-inch washers; 1 adjustable spring tension cafe curtain rod; two 2-inch by #6 wood screws; six 1 1/4-inch by #6 wood screws; twenty 5 penny finishing nails; two 5/16-inch rubber chairleg tips; glue; sandpaper. As you work, follow the diagram and measurements shown in the drawing above.

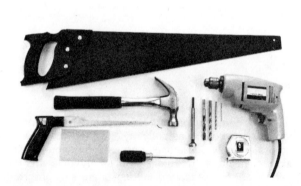

REQUIRED TOOLS are shown in the photo above. They include a hammer; screwdriver; 1/4-inch power drill; 1/8-inch, 5/16-inch, 3/8-inch, and 1/16-inch drill bits; keyhole (three in one) saw with interchangeable blades, or a saber saw with interchangeable blades.

FRAME LOOM parts shown here include 1) cafe rod, 2) adjustable spacer bar, 3) fixed spacer bar, 4) harness supports, 5) harness rods, and 6) heddles. Also see page 16.

How to Build and Use a 4-Harness Frame Loom

Here's a frame loom with a number of good features: it requires only basic woodworking tools for construction, collapses for flat storage, has an adjustable tension bar for control of warp tension and added warp length, utilizes continuous warp for easy warping, and may be used with from one to four harnesses. The harness system creates an excellent shed, and the loom itself may be made up in several sizes to correspond to the dimensions of your work. Though large, it is not excessively heavy or unwieldy.

When choosing your loom dimensions, consider these size factors: the maximum size for this loom is 28½ inches by 36 inches and it will weave a piece 24 inches wide and from 66 inches to 72 inches long; the minimum size is 19½ inches by 25 inches and will produce a piece 14 inches wide and from 45 inches to 50 inches long. The frame width should be 5½ inches greater than the widest warp width; and length should measure one half the minimum warp length plus 3 inches. Have the lumberyard cut the ¾-inch plywood to the proper dimensions (they may charge a small fee for this service).

Dowel sizes correspond to frame width. All four harness dowels should be ½-inch in diameter for frame widths of 23 inches or less and ⅝-inch in diameter for greater frame widths. The adjustable spacer bar dowel should be ⅞-inch in diameter for frames 23 inches wide or narrower and 1 inch in diameter for greater widths. The fixed spacer bar is ¾-inch in diameter, regardless of frame size.

HOW TO MAKE

Refer frequently to photo and diagram on page 14 for measurements and placement guides as you work.

1. Following diagram, measure and mark outline of rectangle to be cut from frame-sized ¾-inch plywood sheet. To begin cutting, drill four 1-inch holes at each corner of rectangle to start keyhole saw; long cuts may be completed with a standard crosscut handsaw. Easiest of all, use a sabersaw for all cuts.

2. On the rectangular piece of ¾-inch plywood removed from loom, squarely mark and cut out two rectangles 6⅛ inches by 3½ inches each for harness supports. (Note: if a frame smaller than 23 inches in width is being constructed, cut these pieces from an extra piece of plywood 12 inches by 36 inches.) Drill three ⅛-inch holes in each harness support (see diagram for placement). Glue and screw supports to side uprights with three 1¼-inch #6 wood screws (see diagram for placement). Screw heads should be flush with surface of wood.

3. Cut ten harness divider bars each 3¼ inches long from ⅝-inch half round moldings. Using sandpaper rolled around a scrap of dowel, form a ¼-inch deep curve in one end of each bar. Drill two ¹⁄₁₆-inch holes in each divider bar as shown in diagram. Use 5-penny nails and white glue to attach divider bars to side uprights, leaving ample space between each divider for harness dowels to slide (¾-inch for ⅝-inch dowels, ⅝-inch for ½-inch dowels).

4. Drill two ⁵⁄₁₆-inch holes into each side upright ⅜-inch below harness support and 1 inch in from each side for carriage bolts. Holding side upright pieces in position next to the frame (see diagram), drill ⁵⁄₁₆-inch holes into frame, using previously drilled holes in the uprights as guides. Enlarge holes in frame to ⅜-inch so carriage bolts will slide easily.

5. Mark positions on both sides of frame for square holes needed for tightening carriage bolt wing nuts. Drill a 1-inch hole into area to be removed, cut out squares with a keyhole saw. Push carriage bolts through uprights and frame, add washers, and tighten down with wing nuts.

6. Cut four harness dowels ¹⁄₁₆-inch shorter than frame width so they will slide easily into slots between harness dividers or rest in indentations on top of dividers.

7. Cut dowel for the fixed spacer bar the same length as the frame width. Drill two ¹⁄₁₆-inch holes through bar 1¼-inch from each end. Thread end of a length of heavy rug wool or carpet yarn through hole at one end and secure with a knot. Wrap yarn closely around this bar from one end to the other. When the spacer bar is covered, tie wool through hole at other end. Coat dowel with a mixture of one part white glue to two parts water and allow to dry overnight. The adjustable spacer bar is made in the same way.

8. Drill a ⅛-inch hole, ¾-inch in from each end of fixed spacer bar for 2-inch #6 wood screws. Holding bar in position along front edge of frame, drill ¹⁄₁₆-inch holes into frame, using previously drilled holes as guides. Screw fixed spacer bar in place.

9. Drill a ⁵⁄₁₆-inch hole through adjustable spacer bar ¾-inch in from each end. Holding bar against top of frame, drill a ⁵⁄₁₆-inch hole ¼-inch into top edge of frame. Using these holes as starting points, continue holes to 2½ inches deep into frame. Be careful to drill hole parallel to edge of frame. Enlarge holes in adjustable spacer bar with a ⅜-inch drill bit.

10. Using a hacksaw blade, cut ⁵⁄₁₆-inch threaded rod into two 10-inch lengths. Turn two wing nuts tightly together on one end of each rod and use to insert rods into holes at end of frame until 7½ inches to 8 inches extend. Remove top wing nut from each rod, slide adjustable spacer bar onto the rods, and replace both wing nuts. Push a rubber tip onto end of each threaded

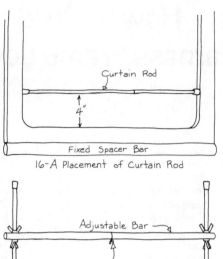

16-A Placement of Curtain Rod

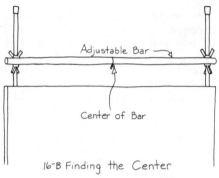

16-B Finding the Center

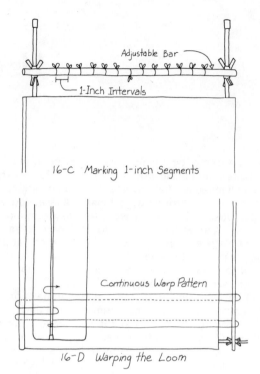

16-C Marking 1-inch Segments

16-D Warping the Loom

EXPANDING *cafe rod* **(16-A)** *forms a turning point for the continuous warp, which is measured, then correctly centered on the loom by a tied string* **(16-B).** *String markers divide spacer bars into 1-inch segments for warping* **(16-C),** *which is accomplished by laying the loom on its side, as shown in* **(16-D).**

rod. (Note: longer rods may be substituted when a longer warp is required.)

11. Using a yardstick, mark portion of the side uprights to be removed so that base of upright will lie flat when loom is tilted forward. Detach uprights and cut off excess wood.

12. Fill cracks and holes with wood putty, sand all edges, and either stain or paint loom body.

13. Adjust length of the cafe curtain rod so that it will spring into position near bottom of rectangular opening in frame.

USING THE FRAME LOOM

Now that the frame loom is built, how does it work? An explanation of the parts of the loom and their functions, then a step by step plan for setting up the loom will help to clear up the mystery. Refer to the photo on page 14 to identify each loom part.

1. Cafe rod. This spring tension rod is braced in the frame and is the meeting point for the continuous warp threads.

2. Adjustable spacer bar. Located at the top of the loom, this bar moves up and down to adjust tension and can add from 5 to 10 extra inches of warp length. Longer-threaded rods may be cut to replace the present rods, making a longer warp possible. The glued yarn wrapping grips warp threads, making the process of warping easier and keeping the threads properly spaced from one another.

3. Fixed spacer bar. Another yarn-wrapped bar at the foot of the loom, this one keeps warp threads evenly spaced apart.

4. Harness supports. These are heavy side boards with a twofold job: to hold up the harness rods and to provide a foot or support for the loom, giving it the proper slant for table top use.

5. Harness rods. Their function is to lift certain warp threads tied to them with string heddles so that the weft may pass unobstructed from selvage to selvage.

6. Heddles. Made from strong string, heddles are secured to the harness rod and looped around certain threads in the warp. When a harness rod is lifted, the string loops lift these warp threads and make a passage for the weft.

Preparing the loom for use is an easy process. You will need the following items: enough yarn to make the proper size of warp (see pages 32 and 33 on Yarn Calculations), a ball of string, tape measure, small plastic ruler, and scissors. Yarn for the warp should be wound into a ball for ease of handling. (Making yarn balls is explained on page 22.)

1. Remove harness rods from loom and then brace the expanding curtain rod in cut opening about 3 to 4 inches up from bottom of loom (16-A). Decide length of your warp and set adjustable spacer bar at proper distance from top edge of loom for that particular warp. The bar should be no closer to top of loom than 2½ inches to allow for loosening of tension if necessary. (If the entire minimum length of warp on loom is not needed for your project, either weave a second piece on remaining warp or use this extra warp for long fringe.)

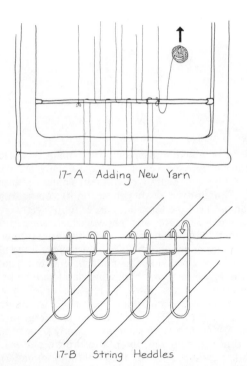

17-A Adding New Yarn

17-B String Heddles

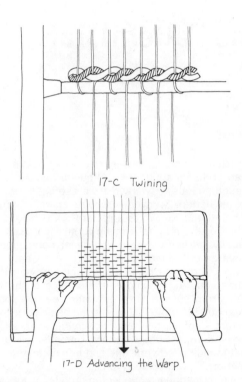

17-C Twining

17-D Advancing the Warp

BEGIN and end each new ball of warp material at the cafe rod to avoid knots in the woven cloth (17-A). String heddles loop around and connect individual warp ends to harness rods (17-B). Twining keeps ends in their proper place and order (17-C). To advance the warp, loosen tension and pull down on cafe rod (17-D).

2. Mark centers of each wrapped bar (16-B), then mentally calculate one half the warp width and mark this distance on either side of center marks. Tie strings to mark where selvages will fall on both bars and then place string markers at 1-inch segments along each bar (16-C). (Example: if spacer bars are 28 inches in length, 14 inches in from one edge would mark the center. A 12-inch wide warp divided by two is 6 inches. String markers are placed 6 inches on either side of center marks, totalling 12 inches. The warp may then be divided into twelve equal 1-inch segments.)

3. Lay the loom on its side, with the front facing you. Tie one end of warp yarn to cafe rod in line with selvage markers and make one complete pass with yarn (16-D). Continue in this way, keeping tension firm and placing correct number of warp threads (called ends) to the inch until warp is completed. If one ball of yarn is not enough to wind on an entire warp, tie it *at the cafe rod* and begin a second ball of yarn at that point (17-A) to complete the warp. When you've finished winding on, tie last warp end at cafe rod.

4. Place loom on its feet, slanting towards you. Drop harness rod 1 into front slot of harness supports and mentally divide warp into groups of four threads. Pick up first thread, or end, in each group of four, passing a length of white paper or cardboard underneath to keep it separate from other ends. Cut a very long piece of string, wind it into a small loose ball, and tie first warp end in each group of four to harness rod 1 by making string loop heddles (17-B). When all are secured, remove harness 1 and let it hang at the cafe rod. Place harness rod 2 in second slot of each sup-

port and attach second warp end in each group of four, following method used for harness 1. Tie up harnesses 3 and 4 in this way. When you've finished, replace all harnesses in their proper harness support slots.

5. Using a small plastic ruler, properly space warp ends on the cafe rod. (Remember that there will be twice as many ends here as at the top or bottom spacer bars.) When all ends are spaced, twine them into place (17-C) until all ends are secure.

6. Give the warp a final check, adjust tension until the threads are firm and lightly flexible, then free cafe rod from loom frame. The warp is now ready to be woven.

To advance the warp, loosen the adjustable spacer bar, releasing warp tension, and pull the cafe rod downward (17-D). After you've finished weaving, remove the rubber tips of the cafe rod, slip it out of the warp, and remove the string heddles by sliding the harness rod out of them. The string may be rewound into a loose ball for future use. The woven piece is then free from the loom. Ideas for finishing, display, and care of your piece are located on pages 24 through 27.

Remember the many ways in which a warp may vary the look of a weaving: by how closely it is set; by how thick the yarn is, or how strong; by the use of different colors, or textures; and many other variations. Experiment with combinations you find interesting; the results will lead to even more ideas and experimentations. For additional information on weaving design and color, turn to pages 37 through 39 where the relationship of warp and weft is discussed in more detail as well as the use of commercial and natural dyes to enhance your weaving projects and ideas.

The Pattern Draft

For certain projects, the weaver uses something much like an architect's blueprint. Although some creations are spontaneous or worked from sketches, others — such as pattern weaves — require specific notation. This notation is known as a pattern draft.

While drafts may take many forms, the basic draft is usually worked out on graph paper containing 8 or 10 squares to the inch. Each square represents either one warp thread (a black square) or one weft thread (a white square) showing on the surface of the fabric (18-A). From such a draft, an entire pattern may be worked out. Most often shown is the basic pattern unit: the number of vertical and horizontal squares comprising one repeat of the pattern. Sometimes a pattern repeat is multiplied vertically and horizontally to show the pattern's progression (18-B).

This information in abbreviated form is the key to any pattern. Needed as well are a threading pattern (which harness lifts which warp ends), a tie-up pattern (what harnesses are lifted together to form part of the pattern), and a treadling pattern (the order in which the harness combinations are lifted to make the pattern). All can be derived from this single square (18-A).

A completed draft would look similar to drawing 18-C. The pattern draft (lower right) represents the woven pattern; the threading order (upper right) represents the harnesses and shows which warp threads are attached to which harnesses; the tie-up (upper left) shows what combinations of the harnesses lifted simultaneously will produce the pattern; and the treadling order at lower left, which may be read from the bottom up or from the top down, shows the order in which these harness combinations are raised to create the pattern as a unit. This information is useful in three ways: 1) You can reproduce almost any pattern based on a draft; 2) You will be able to draft a pattern from threading, tie-up, and treadling information; and 3) You will be able to formulate (and check out on paper) your own ideas for pattern drafts. Drafting is a valuable tool that is well worth learning.

Here is how to derive the necessary information from a pattern draft:

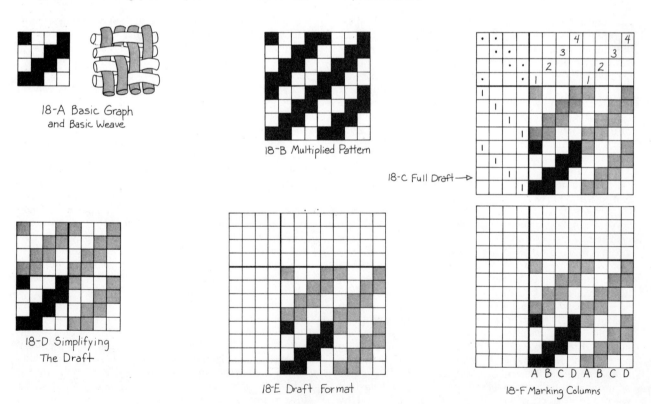

18-A Basic Graph and Basic Weave

18-B Multiplied Pattern

18-C Full Draft →

18-D Simplifying The Draft

18-E Draft Format

18-F Marking Columns

A B C D A B C D

RELATIONSHIPS of warp and weft are more easily understood when reduced to graph form. Figures 18-A through 19-C explain a simple balanced twill pattern by breaking it down into its basic components. Drafts are used as "recipes" when you're working with complicated weave patterns which may require decoding.

1. Simplify the draft down to one multiple of the basic pattern repeat. Darken in or square off the repeat (18-D). (See also figure 18-B.)

2. Extend vertical and horizontal lines to create four distinct areas (18-E).

3. To find a threading pattern, mark the first *vertical* column of the draft, and any other vertical columns that are exactly the same, as A. The next different vertical column is marked B, as well as all other matching vertical columns. Continue to do this until all columns are marked with a letter (18-F).

4. Mark a 1 above all A columns, 2 above all B columns, and so on. This will show which harnesses carry which threads (19-A).

5. Now read across the first *horizontal* row at the *bottom* of the draft. (Drafts may also be worked from the top horizontal row down, but in this case we will be reading from the bottom up.) Threads one and two are the only warp threads raised for this row, thus they are marked with dots in the upper left area of the draft; this is the tie-up (19-B). Place a mark also in front of the first horizontal row (the treadling pattern). This shows that to achieve row one, harnesses one and two are raised simultaneously.

6. Continue as in step 5 to read across the draft. Move up one row at a time, mark the threads to be raised, and directly below, mark the row concerned. When you've finished, the draft should look like figure 19-C. This is a complete draft for this pattern. In order to extend the pattern, repeat the threading as many times as necessary.

This procedure will work for most drafts and is a real key to the complexities of the more intricate weaves.

Copying from a photo or sketch. A photograph or sketch may be the inspiration for a certain weave, but no draft is available. What to do? First, approximately gauge the size (you may count the warp and weft threads if visible), sketch the pictured design as accurately as possible, then transfer the sketch to graph paper (19-D). Proportion the design and block it out by squares to get a basic pattern draft (19-E).

Drafting from a recipe. Pattern recipes are often published in abbreviated form, giving only threading, tie-up, and treadling (19-F). To see the pattern in draft form, sketch out a draft plan on graph paper, fill in the given information, and construct the basic draft (19-G).

Constructing your own drafts. Eventually you'll want to design your own patterns, and for this purpose the draft is a great help. Ideas can be tried out on paper before setting up your loom to weave sample pieces. In this way, any problem areas in the design can be instantly corrected.

Experimentation can be approached in two ways: First, a draft may be drawn in graph form and the technical details for setting it up worked out. Second, a threading, tie-up, and treadling order can be established, then variations in the weaving can be developed on graph paper.

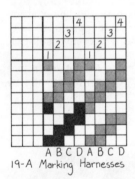
A B C D A B C D
19-A Marking Harnesses

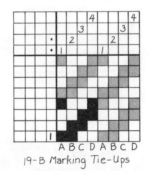
A B C D A B C D
19-B Marking Tie-Ups

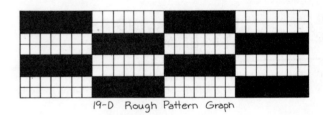
19-D Rough Pattern Graph

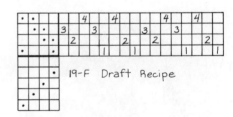
19-F Draft Recipe

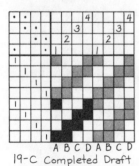
A B C D A B C D
19-C Completed Draft

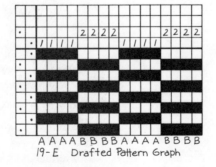
A A A A B B B B A A A A B B B B
19-E Drafted Pattern Graph

19-G Constructed Draft Recipe
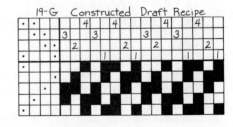

*GRAPHS ALLOW the reconstruction of weaves from a drawing or a photograph (**19-D** and **19-E**), as well as a preview of the final appearance of a draft recipe as taken from any book of weave patterns (**19-F** and **19-G**). Experimentation on paper permits any changes to be easily made ahead of time with just a quick erasure.*

Needleweaving

Needleweaving could easily be called the weaver's sketch pad. A technique that uses a needle to carry weft over and under warp threads, needleweaving is a handy tool for trying out new materials and techniques, color arrangements, or pattern weaves on small cardboard looms before committing them to a larger project.

The weft carrier can range from a bent yarn darning needle to a cording bodkin. Blunt-tipped tapestry needles and handmade butterfly bobbins also work well. Simple looms are usually made from cardboard, masonite, or art board. Other variations include pin or nail looms, shaped looms (see facing page, upper right), hoops, or found object looms. Needleweaving adapts well to use in large woven works when small, irregularly-shaped areas are to be added or where special techniques (such as inlay) or small color additions are wanted.

In working with small tapestry-style weavings, use a cardboard loom upon which a design or pattern has been drawn. Then follow this design when filling in shapes, colors, and textures; beat the weft down with a household fork or haircomb.

NEEDLEWEAVING AS A LEARNING TOOL

The simplicity of the cardboard loom and the availability of the few other necessary tools make needleweaving a good learning tool. It can be taught to almost anyone from school-age children on up. Weaving schools make use of this technique in design workshops, where specific problems are set up and solved in an individual way. Used as a problem solver, the small format needle-woven piece can give new insights into your attitudes toward color and design.

Some of the following ideas have been used successfully for individual study:

• Sketch a landscape, real or imaginary, with colored pencils or pastels; divide the sketch into sections, and develop each section as a separate entity (see facing page, bottom). The sections can either be rejoined or displayed separately.
• Paint your design directly on the warp (see project pages 62 through 64 for a warp painted doll).
• Sketch an object from nature, then choose one square inch of the design, enlarge, and use it for a weaving design.
• Cut up a completed design and weave from the reassembled version.
• Sketch an object, then weave it in texture only.
• Superimpose organic shapes over the linear strictness of warp stripes (see facing page, upper left).
• Interpret yourself in yarn—do a figurative self-portrait (see photo below, right).
• Shape your weaving by changing its outline from a strict rectangle, by building up certain areas, and by working it onto a three-dimensional frame.

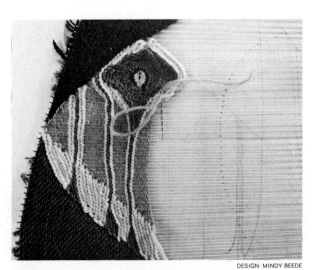

DESIGN: MINDY BEEDE

NEEDLEWEAVING can produce a rich tapestry of weave and texture variations in small areas. Final details and special yarns can be added at the weaver's discretion.

DESIGN: MARTHA KLEIN

TRANSFERRED to the medium of tapestry, this needlewoven "picture" is a self-portrait of the artist. Note the use of tapestry slits and joins (for more information see page 44).

DESIGN: SUSAN STERNLIEB

ORGANIC shapes added by needleweaving give three-dimensional quality to a warp-striped background. This technique creates an effect very similar to embroidery.

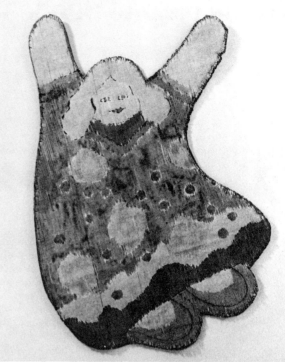

DESIGN: MARI SPEYER AND K. LEE MANUEL

NATURAL FOILS for needleweaving are found in shaped cardboard looms such as this doll, used for the stuffed hand-painted warp pillow project given on page 63.

DESIGN: SUSAN STERNLIEB

INSPIRED by a pastel landscape by the artist, this needlewoven tapestry was constructed from individually woven segments, each a complete entity in its own right. When finished, all were joined into one complete unit. Texture and visual interest were added by the use of nubby yarns in varied colors.

Some Helpful Suggestions

Here are a number of suggestions that will make weaving go even more smoothly. They cover two areas: problem-solving and helpful hints.

PROBLEM-SOLVING

Improper threading sequence. Sometimes when you are threading the loom, you may skip over a warp end or tie it to the wrong harness rod. In the first case, check to see that the entire threading order is correct. If so, remove the thread entirely; if not, re-thread the entire sequence up to the point where the thread was skipped. If the thread is tied to the wrong rod, cut the string loop holding the misthreaded end and tie it to the proper rod *in the right place* with a separate string loop.

Extra warp end. You may find that you have threaded two consecutive threads onto the same harness. This duplication can be corrected by cutting the extra thread in half, securing the two halves where the other warp threads are started and finished (to keep warp tension constant), and then trimming off excess thread.

Uneven warp tension. When some warp ends are tighter or more loose than others, the weft will look uneven and wavey; sometimes the weaving edge will have a slight diagonal angle to it. This can be prevented by giving even, proper tension to all warp ends when warping the loom. Correcting tension after a weaving has been started is a nuisance but can be done by using small squares of cardboard, matchsticks, or folded pieces of paper. Push them under the loose warp threads at the top of the loom and adjust them until the tension is even across the warp. They will have to be repositioned each time the warp is advanced, so it is best to establish even tension at the very beginning.

Broken warp end. Breaking warp ends usually indicate either too much tension or a weak warp material. If you must use a material not really suitable for warping, keep the tension more loose than normal. If an end does break, cut a new warp thread the length that remains to be woven plus a few extra inches. Remove the broken thread, and replace it as shown in drawing 22-A.

Streaks in the weft. Some of the woven portion of the cloth might have the appearance of being darker or lighter than surrounding areas; this is caused by uneven beating, raising harnesses in the wrong order, or using yarns of the same color but taken from different dye lots. Try to keep color, harness order, and beating pressure constant.

Selvage problems. This can mean weft loops at the selvage, a wavy edge, or selvage warp ends that have frayed or broken apart. Loops and waviness will be corrected through practice; drawing in too much causes broken selvage warp ends by putting undue tension and friction on them. Repair them immediately in the same way as broken warp ends.

A twill weave may occasionally present selvage problems due to its unbalanced weave. If, when the shed is changed, the weft is in the same position above or below the first selvage thread, as in the previous weft pass, correct this as shown in drawing 23-A.

HELPFUL HINTS

Making yarn balls. A convenient form for the yarn ball is the pull-skein version. It's wrapped so that the free end can be pulled from the center, not the outside, of the ball. This means the yarn ball will not roll about when being unwound. First, fold a small square of paper twice in the same direction, then grasp one end of the yarn with this folded paper and wrap the yarn around the paper, keeping one end of the folded paper free. When the yarn is wound, remove the paper. The ball will now pull from the center (see drawing 23-B).

The butterfly bobbin. Used for tapestry, inlay, and hand-manipulated weaves, the butterfly bobbin is

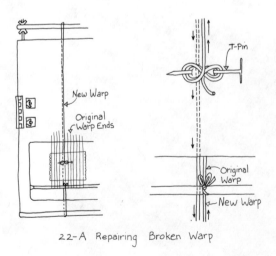

22-A Repairing Broken Warp

TRIM OFF and secure broken warp and all loose ends at the cafe rod. Tie new end at cafe rod and attach to woven cloth looped around a T-pin as shown above (22-A).

wound around the fingers of one hand and secured with a double half hitch knot as shown in drawing 23-C.

Keeping repeat areas even. If you plan to weave two lengths of fabric and then join them at the selvages, any repeats or pattern areas across each piece must match up at the edges. Keep these areas equal by cutting cardboard strips to the length of each repeat area and measuring the repeats against these strips frequently as the weaving progresses. If you follow this procedure the edges should match correctly.

Measuring the length of a weaving in progress. Use a flexible tape measure to check the length of a woven piece as it is being woven, adding colored string or safety pins at every foot. Be sure to make the measurement with tension slightly released.

Weaving with more than one shuttle or more than one color. Colors can either be wound onto a single shuttle and passed as a group, or wound onto separate shuttles and passed in sequence to achieve a particular color or textural effect. When using more than one shuttle, start each of them from the same side. As a

shuttle is passed, lay it on the woven surface of the cloth with each succeeding shuttle placed above the previous one. Always use the bottom shuttle in the row, placing it at the top when finished as shown in drawing 23-D. In this way all weft will be locked at the selvages.

Making woven samples and keeping records. It is a good investment of time to file photos or slides of pieces you have woven, samples of various yarns, ideas for future projects, and other important information. Keep finished swatches of every piece you have made (the swatch may be taken from a length of extra warp added to the total warp required for the project) with information on technique, materials, pattern, color arrangements, problems, and solutions attached to the back of the sample, for you may want to duplicate or elaborate on a certain project at a later date.

Another helpful assist is given by yarn cards from supply houses; they show at a glance which yarns are available for use. All of these materials should be kept where they can be easily located at any time. Cardboard file boxes, good for this purpose, are sold by stationers or office supply stores.

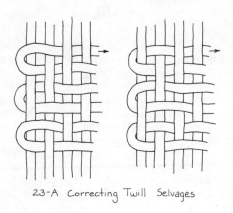

23-A Correcting Twill Selvages

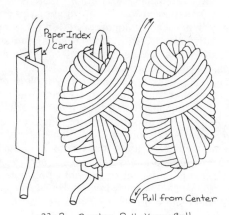

23-B Center Pull Yarn Ball

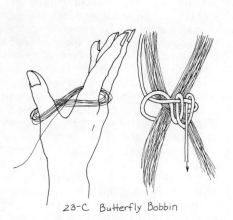

23-C Butterfly Bobbin

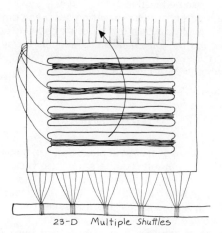

23-D Multiple Shuttles

TWILL SELVAGES (23-A) need to be corrected occasionally because of variances in their weave patterns. Yarn balls (23-B) pull from the center and won't unravel as you are working with them. This comes in handy when winding bobbins or continuous warps. Butterfly bobbins are wound from index finger to thumb and secured with a double half hitch knot (23-C). Keep selvages smooth by correctly locking in any weft floats (23-D).

The Final Touch

There's a lot more to weaving than designing and making a piece; it must be suitably finished, well displayed, and occasionally cleaned to retain a really professional appearance.

FINISHING

The design of your woven piece will determine the finishing techniques to be used. A particular finish should be decided upon at the same time that the weaving itself is planned so that everything will work together properly when the piece is completed. If you wait until the very end, there may not be enough yarn left to finish it properly, or there could be too much left over, resulting in cut off and wasted yarn. Fringe, beads, macrame, hemming, and other methods can be adapted to your design to create a unified, complete look. Many things can be incorporated into the finish of a piece; they can be ready-made (beads), found objects (shells, seeds, leaves, and such), or hand-made (pompons, clay beads, crochet balls).

Finishing also includes tucking in any broken ends; washing, steaming, ironing, or drycleaning the piece; and clipping or brushing the surface, if necessary. Tuck any dangling threads into the body of the piece, using a tapestry needle or crochet hook (see photo 25-A). Some items, especially linen and woolens, should be immersed in warm to hot water, rinsed, and pressed while damp to shrink the fabric (do not wring out—this forms wrinkles). Clothing yardage, curtains, or upholstery material can be brushed off and sent to the dry cleaners for professional pressing and shrinking.

Tapestries, wall hangings, or warp-faced and weft-faced rugs can be finished in two ways. Brushing gives a fuzzy appearance; damp-pressing sharpens outlines. Pile rugs usually require only a brisk shaking out.

Techniques for joining fabrics, finishing hems, and making a variety of fringes are shown on pages 25, 26, and 27, photos 25-A through 27-F.

DISPLAY

This is another aspect of your piece that can be planned ahead of time but left flexible enough to be changed should you develop another idea. If you know where the weaving will be displayed, key the design and colors to its surroundings. Do the same for anything that will be used as wearing apparel; consider the purpose to which the item will be put, then think of the personality and coloring of the person who will wear your weaving creations.

If the weaving is three-dimensional, it can be placed on a pedestal or stand, hung from the ceiling, or extended from the wall. Think about integrating it into a grouping of indoor plants or an established sculpture display. Scale it to its setting for best results.

A wall hanging can be displayed still attached to the frame on which it was woven, suspended from a dowel or branch, framed like a painting, or hung from wires or concealed hooks. If it will be seen, the material used for hanging a weaving should suit the mood of its design. Plexiglass and metal are clean and graphic; branches, found objects, or metal rings are rustic.

Rugs can cover the floor or warm up a wall, drape a sofa, or hang from a balcony. Casual pillows will look just as attractive scattered about as placed carefully on a couch or chair.

Well-displayed weaving will add a custom-made look to your home of inviting warmth and casual elegance.

CARE

Weavings hold up very well under use, but once in a while a thorough cleaning will help them to look their best and to last longer.

Some pieces that don't receive much wear (wall hangings and sculpture) can be shaken out to remove dust. If colors have dulled due to surface dirt, a damp cloth run over the surface will restore the original luster. Should a hanging or tapestry become really dirty, immersion in warm, soapy water will lift out soil. Be sure to rinse thoroughly and pat with a terry cloth towel to remove excess water before laying the piece out flat to dry. Fragile or rough-textured weavings should be cleaned in this way or sent to dry cleaners.

Rugs should be professionally cleaned. If you are particularly concerned about a rug, send it to a specialist, such as an Oriental rug cleaner and restorer.

Garments made from woolen yardage should be drycleaned. Small spots can be removed at home, but overall cleaning is best left to the professionals. If made from cotton, linen, or synthetics, an article of clothing can be hand-laundered at home in warm, soapy water, rinsed, and laid out *flat* to dry. If you want the article to retain its original shape, draw a rough outline of it on wrapping paper before washing. Afterwards, adjust the garment until it fits the original outline, pin it into place, and allow to dry.

When care is taken with woven articles, they should last indefinitely. If you plan to store a weaving for any length of time, protect it from damage by carefully folding, then wrapping it in tissue paper. Woolens should be stored with a handful of mothballs or eucalyptus seed pods. Rugs should never be folded but rolled up lengthwise with the face inward; a broomstick or large dowel can be used as a core for wrapping them. Try to completely cover the rolled-up rug with a large plastic or canvas sheet.

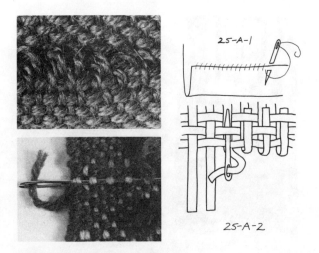

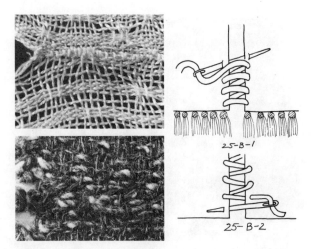

FINISHED or unfinished raw edges may be hemmed with an overhand stitch **(25-A-1)** or run back into the cloth one or two at a time with a tapestry needle **(25-A-2)**.

JOINING two lengths of cloth can be accomplished by the use of an overhand stitch **(25-B-1)** or by an interlocking stitch similar to that used to lace shoes **(25-B-2)**.

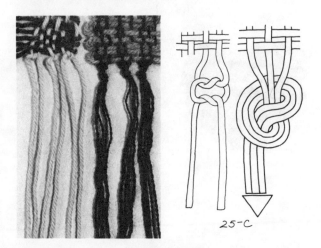

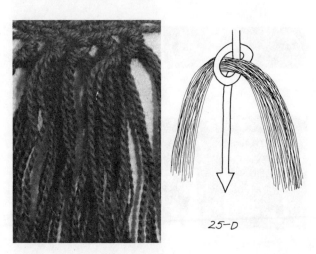

PAIRS OF FRINGE may be square knotted **(above, left)** or overhand knotted **(above, right)** to prevent unwoven edges or groups of fringe from unraveling.

ADDED FRINGE gives weight to a sparse warp. Bundles of yarn cut to twice the length of original fringe add density when overhand knotted into place **(above)**.

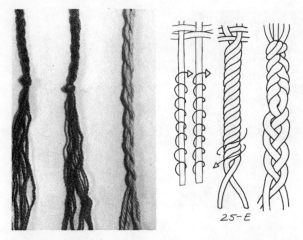

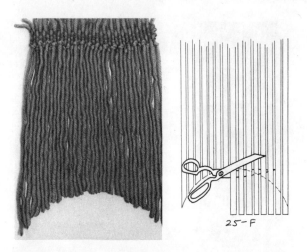

BRAIDS and plied fringe are good ways to secure unfinished warp ends of a project. Twist ends each to the left and then to the right for plying. Braid as shown in the drawing.

SHAPE FRINGE by making a cardboard or paper pattern to lay underneath. Cut along this outline with a very sharp scissors for a smooth well-shaped edge.

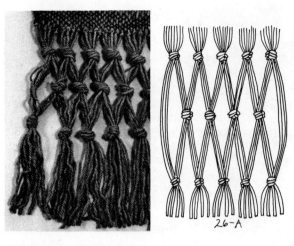  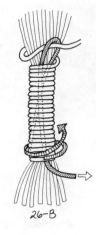

*MACRAME TRIM **(above)** results from groups of overhand knotted fringe alternately resplit and reknotted several times to create an open, lace-like appearance.*

*WRAPPING GROUPS of fringe **(above)** gives an Indian braid appearance to trim. Use brightly colored contrasting yarns for wrapping, alternating them to make stripes.*

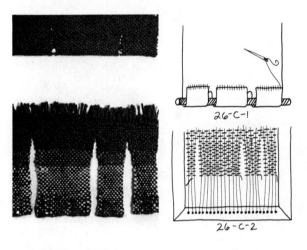  

*WOVEN FRINGE can be hemmed to hold a weighted dowel **(26-C-1)** or left plain **(26-C-2)** as tab-like scallops. Separate groups of fringe before weaving them.*

*HEART **(above)** was made on a shaped pin loom, and so has no unwoven edges. Such pieces can be appliqued onto other woven articles or jeans for accent.*

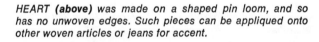

 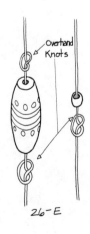 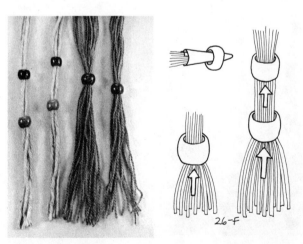

BEADS in a variety of sizes are randomly knotted onto fringe with an overhand knot. Dimension and texture are thus added to an otherwise flat weaving element.

GROUPS OF FRINGE can be wrapped with heavy paper wound to a point and threaded as a group through large beads with wide holes for an Indian-braid effect.

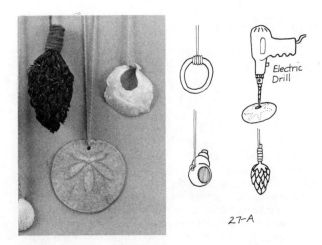

27-A

27-B

FOUND OBJECTS, such as shells or seed pods, add visual interest when knotted or wrapped onto the fringe **(above)**. Use a drill with a small bit to make holes.

FEATHERS can be used alone or mixed in with other objects as a soft accent trim **(above)**. Use the technique for wrapping fringe (page 26) to attach feathers.

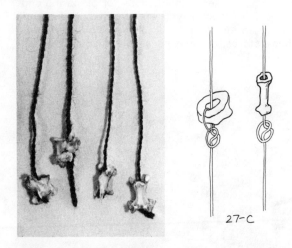

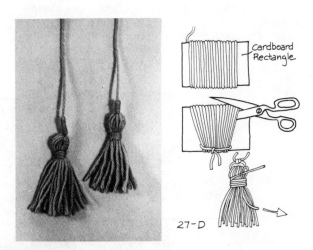

27-C

27-D

CHICKEN neckbones **(above)**—or any other small bones— make interesting beads. Boil the bones to loosen any meat left on them, then place in sunlight to dry before using.

YARN TASSELS **(above)** are first wrapped around cardboard, then knotted at one edge and cut on the other. The center is then wrapped as with wrapped fringe (page 26).

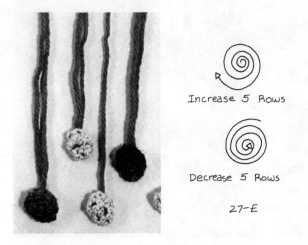

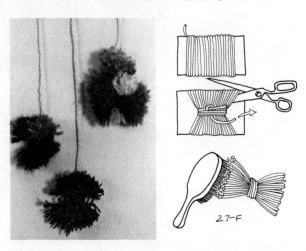

27-E

27-F

CROCHET BALLS are made by chaining 5 rows of single crochet around the first crochet loop, then reversing the order back down to one final crochet loop.

POMPONS form thick tassels with 2 brushes. Tie with one piece of yarn for puff-ball appearance; wrap with several strands for sheaf look. Comb to add a fuzzy appearance.

Floor Looms and How They Work

Foot-operated floor looms are probably the most common type of loom used by advanced weavers today. They streamline weaving by utilizing the feet to lift harnesses, thereby freeing the hands to concentrate on passing the weft. This adds speed and rhythm to the process. In addition, a large, attached beater swings forward to press each weft pass into place. A technical advance over the small hand-held beater, it imparts greater accuracy and uniformity to the beat and weft density, and also keeps selvages even. The tempo and control imparted by a floor loom encourages the weaver to attempt longer yardage and more complicated projects.

Study the photos below and compare floor loom parts to the parts of the four-harness frame loom on page 14. You will find that individual parts, though different in appearances, have very similar functions. Frame loom harness rods and floor loom harnesses have the same function, as do string loop heddles and wire heddles. Some of the functions, however, are approached in different ways: for example, the method of advancing the warp. But if you understand the four-harness frame loom, you will not be confused by a floor loom.

The following three pages will give a fairly detailed explanation of how floor looms work, but this is far from a complete set of instructions for preparing and using the floor loom. If you wish to study the use of foot-operated looms in depth, check with local libraries, book stores, or weaving supply shops. They will

COUNTERBALANCE loom and how it works is briefly explained on page 29. Parts include 1) breast beam, 2) cloth beam, 3) beater, 4) reed, 5) harnesses, 6) heddles, 7) treadles, 8) warp beam, 9) back beam, 10) apron rod and apron.

probably carry a number of books devoted entirely to that subject. Our main objective here is to introduce you to the floor loom as a potential weaving tool, should you ever wish to use one.

LOOM TYPES

Although many styles and types of floor looms are used for weaving, the classification can be generalized into two types that you are most likely to see. They are the counterbalance loom and the jack loom. Each has specific characteristics that make it unique and particularly adaptable to certain uses.

Counterbalance loom

Strong and more inexpensively made than most floor looms, the counterbalance is a loom that has been in use since Colonial times. Most early American families spun yarn from flax, wool, or cotton, then wove their own cloth on these looms, often built by a member of the family.

The name *counterbalance* comes from the method of raising and lowering the harnesses. Two harnesses are connected by cords that run up to, over, and around pulleys or rollers at the top of the loom. Each harness is connected to a separate pedal at the bottom of the loom. When the weaver steps on one pedal, it pulls its harness down. As this occurs, the cords over the pulleys lengthen on this side and shorten on the other, raising the second harness. Expressed in weaver's terms, each harness counterbalances the other (see drawing 30-A).

The pulley system makes treadling the pedals very easy because a portion of the weight of the rising harness is supported by the cords and pulleys. Since the concept requires pairs of harnesses in order for the pulley system to work, this loom is most often made with two or four harnesses.

Because alternating harnesses rise and drop at the same time, the warp at the front of the loom must pass through the center of the reed (instead of resting on the shuttlerace). This is called a *sinking shed* because the harness attached to the treadle being pressed sinks downward. The shed formed is very large and excellent for warps under heavy tension, such as those used in making rugs and tapestries; it produces less stretch

LOW PROFILE jack loom is discussed on page 30, followed by a simplified explanation of how the loom is used. Parts are 1) breast beam, 2) cloth beam, 3) beater, 4) reed, 5) harnesses, 6) heddles, 7) treadles, 8) warp beam, 9) back beam, 10) apron rod and apron, 11) lams, 12) tie-up cords.

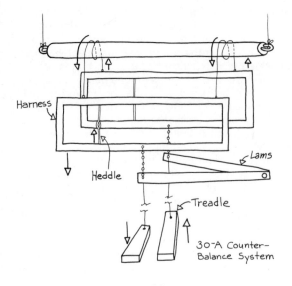

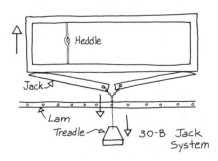

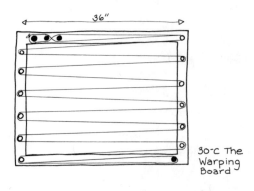

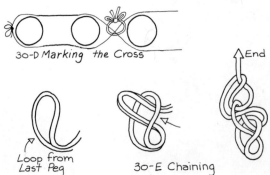

DRAWINGS above describe counterbalance system **(30-A)**, jack system **(30-B)**, warping board and sequence **(30-C)**, warp cross and chaining **(30-D and 30-E)**.

in a highly tensioned warp, reducing the chance of breakage in the warp threads.

Though any pattern using a balanced number of harnesses can be made on the counterbalance, weaves that require three harnesses to rise or drop against one harness are difficult at best.

Jack loom

Instead of working on an overhead pulley system, this loom functions on the principle of jacking up, or lifting, each harness independently. Harnesses can be raised from below by pressing down on a treadle. This pulls down on the lam connected at the centerpoint of a pair of jacks; the jacks rise at the outside, lifting the harness (see drawing 30-B, at left). A second jack system: the lam pulls down on a set of chains at the outside of the loom that run up to an overhead support. The chains in turn trip a triangular jack that fits the harness from above.

On the jack loom, several harnesses may be attached to each treadle, making the building up of a pattern simple enough to be controlled with only one foot: i.e., for a simple twill, harnesses 1 and 2 can be attached to one treadle, 2 and 3 to a second treadle, 3 and 4 to a third, 4 and 1 to a fourth. As each treadle is pushed down, only those harnesses attached to it will rise; the rest remain stationary. Because each jack system works independently of the others, both balanced and unbalanced weaves are possible.

At the reed, the warp rides on the base along the shuttlerace. When a shed is opened, all warp controlled by moving harnesses rises upward while the stationary warp remains along the shuttlerace. This provides a smooth tensioned surface to support the shuttle as it is thrown from side to side.

HOW THE FLOOR LOOM WORKS

Placing a warp onto a floor loom (also called *threading* or *dressing* the loom) can be done in several ways. We will explain only the most simple method as an illustration of preparing the loom for weaving.

How to prepare the warp. A warping board (drawing 30-C) is used to count and measure out individual warp lengths. There are usually 36 inches between pegs, since warp measurement is usually figured in yards. Yarn is tied to the first peg at the upper left hand side of the board, then passed *over* the second peg and *under* the third. The yarn then goes back and forth along the face of the board in a way that will make the correct length of warp for a particular project. At the last peg, the yarn turns to repeat its path back to the beginning peg, crossing *over* the third peg and *under* the second peg on its return (see drawing 30-C). This makes a *cross* between the second and third pegs, a step which is important for keeping warp threads in the order in which they are wound. To continue, the warp thread goes back around the first peg and repeats the sequence exactly.

When the desired number of warp ends have been wound, the yarn returns to the first peg and is tied. The cross is retained by tying a string securely through it (drawing 30-D). Then the warp is removed by chaining (drawing 30-E).

Threading the warp onto the loom. The string securing the cross is replaced by lease rods, which are tied between the breast beam and the stationary beater. The cross now gives the correct order of the threads for sleying, or entering the warp into the reed. The chain is loosely tied to the beam with a string to prevent its unraveling, then the reed is marked at its center and at the points where the edges of the woven piece will fall. Next, each warp thread is drawn through the reed from front to back with a sley hook (drawing 31-A).

When all threads have been drawn through the reed, each is passed through one heddle of one harness in the order indicated by the threading plan for the chosen pattern (drawing 31-B—see also pages 18 and 19 for Pattern Drafting). After the heddles are threaded, the warp ends are tied in groups to the back beam apron rod with a square knot (drawing 31-C).

Winding on the warp. For this step it's better to have two people, one to keep order and tension in the warp at the front of the loom and one to turn the warp beam. The warp is combed with the fingers to remove tangles until the beater and reed can be drawn forward to rest on the breast beam. Then the warp is divided in half and held taut in each hand.

The warp beam is slowly turned by crank, beginning the winding on process. As the warp is wound, the beater moves with the yarn until it reaches the harness support. At this point, the winding stops until the yarn can be combed and tightened again. Then the process is repeated until all of the warp is wound on except two feet. As the threads are wound around the warp beam, brown paper, corrugated cardboard, or flat sticks are added to separate one layer of warp from the next.

At the front of the loom, warp ends are tied in small groups to the cloth beam apron rod with a half square knot (drawing 31-C). Tension is then evenly adjusted across the warp and the square knots are completed.

Attaching the harnesses to the treadles. Each lam is joined to one harness and provides a point at which the treadle and harness may be connected. Treadles can operate more than one harness, so each harness lam is tied to the proper treadle by a cord or chain to match the tie-up order of the pattern being used (drawing 31-D).

WEAVING ON THE FLOOR LOOM

Pressing down on the treadles starts the process of weaving by opening a shed. The shed is then cleared by moving the beater forward and back. Next, the shuttle is thrown and the pick beaten into place. The process is then repeated as the treadles are pressed down in the order predetermined by a pattern draft. For information on pattern drafting, see page 18.

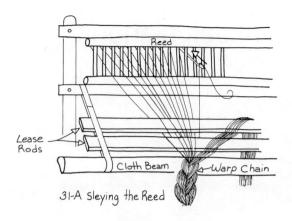

31-A Sleying the Reed

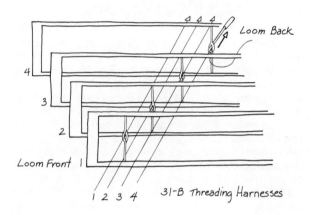

31-B Threading Harnesses

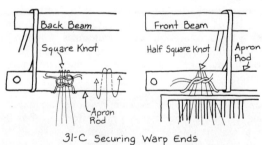

31-C Securing Warp Ends

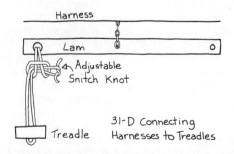

31-D Connecting Harnesses to Treadles

SLEYING the reed (31-A) and the heddles (31-B), tying onto the back and front beam apron rods (31-C), and joining lams to treadles (31-D) are shown above.

Yarn Calculations

Deciding on the amount of yarn necessary for a particular project doesn't have to be guesswork. Certain formulas exist that will greatly simplify the task.

ESTIMATING YARN SIZES AND WEIGHTS

To determine the number of yards contained in any given form of a yarn sold commercially is often a problem. Weights are usually given, for these are the specifics required for knitting, crocheting, and other fiber-related crafts. This leaves the weaver to guess at the amount of yarn he is purchasing, since yarns can come in cones, balls, skeins, tubes, pull-skeins, twists, and other variations, and weights per package can range from a fraction of an ounce to several pounds. Shopkeepers may be able to tell you how many yards a certain package contains, but it is good to be able to work this out for yourself. Another point to remember: try to buy all yarn for one color from the same dye lot. Different dye lots can vary, causing slight color changes in the yarn.

All yarn production is measured by standard systems of weights and measures, and if no yardage amount is given on a package, an approximate amount may be figured by using this information. Synthetic yarns duplicating the appearance and size of yarns from the following groups may be figured as belonging to the group, but synthetics in other forms must be roughly estimated.

Cotton: The standard measurement for cotton is called a hank, and a number 1 hank/1 ply cotton yarn has 840 yards to the pound. As the size numbers increase, the yarn becomes finer and the number of yards to the pound becomes greater. Number 10 one ply has ten times 840 yards, or 8400 yards to the pound. Plied yarns are indicated by a slash mark, as 10/2, or two strands of number 10 yarn plied or wound together. Yardage per pound for plied yarn is figured by multiplying the yarn size number by 840 (number of yards per pound for number 1/1 ply) and then dividing the results by the number of plys. 10/2 yarn would be twice as heavy and would have about half of the yardage per pound of 10/1 yarn. Spun silk and rayon often use the cotton system.

Silk: When not based on the cotton hank system, silk is measured by the denier, a weight equivalent to .05 gram. A number 1 denier/1 ply silk filament would have 4,464,528 yards to the pound. The denier system is the only measurement where, as the size numbers grow greater, the yarn correspondingly becomes larger, so silk usually comes in much larger size numbers, as in number 1000/one ply, which contains 4465 yards to the pound. When based on the cotton hank system, the silk ply system is also unique, for a change in the number of plies in a particular size of silk yarn does not change the weight. Yarns *one half* the size of the finished yarn are plied to create it; for example, two plies of number 2000 ply silk filament are twisted together to make a number 1000/2 ply yarn, leaving the yarn weight for all number 1000 plies constant. Size numbers for silk are often given in two numbers, as in number 800/1000, 2 ply. Because of variations in size of this natural fiber, only a size approximation can be offered.

Wool. Since two types of wool yarn are produced, there are also two measuring standards:
Woolens. This yarn unit is called either a cut or a run. The Philadelphia system gives 300 yards of 1 cut/1 ply woolen yarn to the pound; the American system gives 1600 yards of 1 run/1 ply woolen yarn to the pound. Size numbers and ply information are the same as for cotton, except that you figure on either 300 or 1600 yards per pound for the standard.
Worsted. The worsted unit, or count, measures 560 yards to one pound of 1 ply/1 count worsted yarn. For this yarn only, the ply number is given before the size number, as in 2/10 (2 ply number 10 count worsted yarn). Again, size and ply information duplicate those of cotton but use 560 yards per pound as a standard.

Linen. A lea of 1 ply linen gives 300 yards to the pound. The same cotton size and ply formulas are used for linen except that you substitute 300 yards per pound as a standard.

ESTIMATING THE WARP

Shaped looms. It is better to estimate the warp yardage for a shaped loom, since these warp lengths vary greatly. Measure each warp length with a ruler or tape measure, then add together for a total length.

Cardboard and frame looms. The warp length is determined by the distance between the nails or notches at the top of the loom and those at the bottom. Multiply the number of nails or notches along the top edge by the warp length to find the total length of yarn needed. Always add one or two yards extra for take-up and possible error.

Table, floor, and 4-harness frame looms. These warps are figured from definite formulas. Although both table and floor looms may have many yards of warp wound on, the 4-harness frame loom warp length ranges from twice the length of the loom to anywhere from 6 inches to 50 inches greater. This variation is possible due to the interchangeable spacer bar rods which add warp length.

First, determine how long the warp should be. A good rule of thumb is to start with the finished length desired for the woven piece, plus about ¼ yard on the 4-harness frame loom for waste. This is the length of extra yarn needed 1) to tie the warp on at the beginning and end and 2) to add enough extra yarn for fringe, trim, and waste. Another ¼ yard should be added for take-up, for the warp will eventually shorten from passing over and under the many crossing weft picks. Sometimes extra yarn is also added so that the weaver may experiment with a design before work on a project. Be sure to express the total length in yards.

Next, determine the total warp width. This is the finished width desired for your piece, plus up to 1 inch at either selvage to counteract possible drawing in. Count the number of ends in 1 inch and multiply this by the total number of inches in the warp width to figure the total number of warp ends. Multiply this by the length of the warp expressed in yards; the answer will be the total number of yards required for the warp. In simplified form the formula reads: ends per inch (epi) x width in inches (w) x length in yards (l) = total warp yardage. To figure warp yardage for a floor loom project, use this formula but add one-third yard for waste, one-third for take-up, and one-third for experimentation.

You can use the following two methods to figure for a warp using more than one color:

1) Because color arrangements are frequently placed in sequences, count the number of threads in a sequence and divide the total number of warp ends by this amount to find the number of sequences across the warp. Count the number of ends of one color in one sequence, then multiply this number by the total number of sequences to find the total number of warp ends for this one color. Repeat until all colors have been figured. Finally, multiply each color total by the length of the warp to get the total yardage needed for each individual color. Here is the simplified formula: total warp ends x ends in one sequence = number of sequences. Single sequence end count for color A x number of sequences x length of warp = total yardage for color A.

2) When there is no set sequence, colors will have to be figured separately. Count each color end called for in the warp, then multiply by the length of the warp. Remember to add a little extra to your final figure, for single color ends have to be tied to the preceding and following colors when a continuous warp is being wound. This is the formula: total color ends x total warp length + tie-in or waste = total color yardage.

Selvages. If selvages of another yarn type are to be added, the amount of yardage needed is figured as total selvage ends x total warp length = total selvage yardage. Selvage additions should be at least two threads on each side of the weaving.

ESTIMATING THE WEFT

This measurement, based on a small cardboard sampler, is the same for all loom types. Cut a 4 inch by 10 inch rectangle of heavy cardboard and notch it according to the number of warp ends per inch. Warp the center 2 inches of the board with the warp yarn you've selected, then weave in the weft materials to be used, one at a time, in the weave pattern or style that will be used and set it at the density desired. Weave 1 inch, then count the number of picks per inch and multiply this number by the warped width of the piece, then by the length to be woven with this particular color or pattern for the number of yards of weft needed. Repeat until all yarns to be used have been figured.

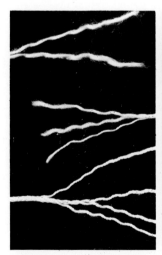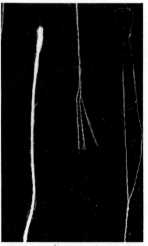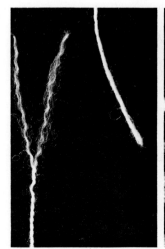

YARNS of different types also come in different plies. At left are two, three, and four ply cottons; at left center are one, two, and three ply silks; at center right are one and two ply worsteds; and at right are one, two, and four ply woolens. The number of plies in a yarn affects its diameter, except in the case of silk.

Yarns, Design, and Color

Just as essential as the warp and weft relationships of a weave are the yarns themselves. The range of types, colors, sizes, and textures is incredibly great — so great, in fact, that it would take years to weave one pattern using each of the fibers or filaments only once for warp and once for weft. This amazing palette allows the weaver to choose materials with just the right characteristics for any particular weaving (see photos, page 35).

WHERE YARN COMES FROM

No matter what the original material, natural or synthetic, it must be spun or drawn into a continuous pliable strand for the purpose of weaving. Wool is sheared from sheep; hair is combed from goats, rabbits, and dogs; cotton is picked; and linen and other bast fibers (such as ramie and jute) are cut, soaked, and beaten. Once these materials have been collected, they are cleaned, combed to lie parallel, and twisted (or spun) into continuous lengths. Silk and synthetics are produced in a slightly different manner: silk is reeled off the cocoon, then plied together to make a filament; synthetics are based on chemical changes that first transform a solid mass to a liquid and then draw the liquid out into a solid filament.

This is a greatly simplified explanation of yarn production; the many intermediate steps in the preparation of each fiber make for fascinating further study.

Of the natural fibers, there are three kinds: animal, vegetable, and mineral in content. Synthetic fibers are chemically produced from both vegetable and mineral sources.

Animal fibers

Wool. Probably the one fiber most used and appreciated by the weaver, wool is easily spun, dyed, and woven. It is light, warm, springy, highly absorbent, wrinkle-resistant, and soft; however, it can shrink when plunged into hot water. Two types of yarn are spun from wool: wool worsted, a smooth, exceptionally strong yarn; and woolen, which has a fuzzy, soft, uncombed appearance.

Hair. Taken from the camel, goat, llama, rabbit, or dog, hair is combed out of the soft undercoat. It is generally blended with wool to add warmth and softness of touch, making it an ideal material for clothing. Other hairs, particularly those of the horse and cow, are coarse and scratchy; their use is generally limited to rugs or sculptural constructions.

Silk. As the story goes, silk was discovered by an Oriental princess taking tea in her garden, when a silkworm cocoon dropped from an overhead branch into the teacup and began to unravel. Fed on mulberry leaves, the silkworm prepares a cocoon for its metamorphosis into a moth; before the moths can emerge, the cocoons are dropped into hot water and the loosened silk is reeled off, several strands at a time, to make a filament. Later the filament is twisted and plied together into a strong silk thread. Silk may also take the form of tussah, or wild silk, reeled from silkworms that are fed from oak and other trees. Another grade of silk is spun from the short fibers of broken cocoons.

Vegetable fibers

Cotton. Preceded only by linen in history, cotton has been a favorite of weavers for centuries. Due to a natural twist in the fiber, which is taken from the seed pod of the plant, spinning is easy, especially when the fiber is wet. It remains stable under heat and tension, dyes well, and can take a variety of sizes, textures, and finishes. Mercerizing is a special treatment that adds strength and luster to the cotton fiber.

Linen. Called a bast fiber, linen is stripped from the stalk of the flax plant. The especially long strands of flax fiber make a yarn that is strong, smooth-surfaced, and lint-free. Although linen is hard to dye and may wrinkle easily, its beauty grows greater with age and wear. Yarn made from the long fibers is called *line;* broken fibers are spun into *tow.*

Ramie. One of the oldest fibers known—and the longest-lasting—ramie has become more readily available because of improved processing methods. Produced from a nettle plant called China Grass, ramie is the strongest of all natural fibers, though very thin and light in weight. Quick-drying and rot-resistant, it has luster, but little elasticity.

Jute. A prickly rough surface gives jute great tactile appeal, in spite of its many drawbacks. The fiber dyes well, but its colors aren't permanent, it is difficult to bleach, it has little strength and no elasticity, and can rot unless chemically treated.

Hemp. From the Philippines and Africa comes hemp, a stiff, relatively shiny, heavy fiber most frequently used for ropes and twine.

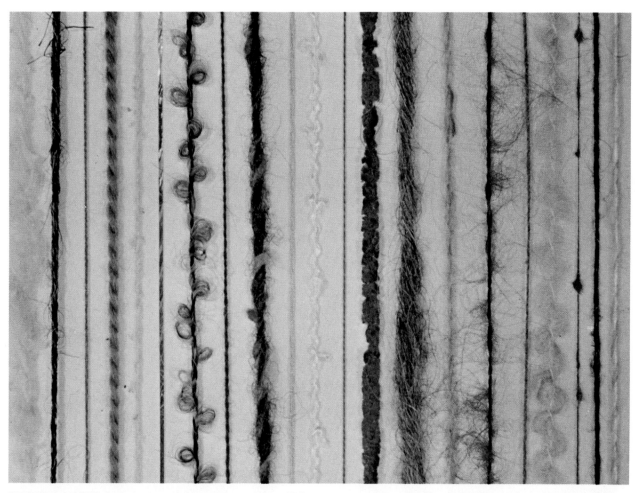

WEAVING YARNS include from left to right: tussah silk/ rayon, horsehair, wetspun linen, English rug wool, Italian noil silk, French gold metallic, loop mohair, wool worsted, English worsted tweed, tussah silk, rayon bouclé, Egyptian cotton, rayon chenille, Icelandic wool, wool tweed fleck, brushed mohair novelty, homespun tweed, orlon nub, douppioni silk, dry spun linen, and slub linen/rayon flake. These yarns are but a small portion of all weaving yarns available.

MORE FIBERS to weave with (left to right): Turkish handspun cotton, silk, linen/rayon flake, flax, cotton chenille, Mexican handspun wool.

ADDITIONAL MATERIALS (left to right): goat hair, raffia, ramie, metallic supported thread, unplied orlon, woolen nub, knitting worsted.

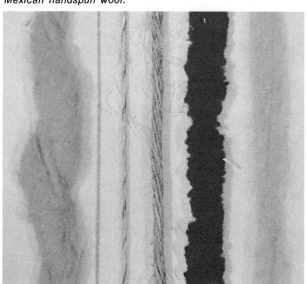

Raffia. Leaf strips from the African palm are processed and dyed to make a material most often used for mats, baskets, hats, and purses. Raffia is flexible, strong, and durable, even when wet.

Reeds, slats, wood strips, bamboo, etc. These and other fibers can be used directly from nature, unprocessed and in dried or raw form.

Mineral fibers

Fiberglas. Often used for upholstery, curtains, or wallcoverings, fiberglas is drawn and quickly spun from hot glass. It dyes very well and won't fade, stain, wrinkle, or burn.

Metallic yarns. Metal yarns have been in use a long time—for centuries, in fact. Today they are most often made from colored aluminum foil that has been cut into strips. These strips may be used by themselves or wrapped around a rayon or silk core to give them strength and support. Some metallics are plastic coated to prevent tarnishing.

Synthetic (man-made) fibers

Rayon and Acetate. Cellulose, which comes from wood pulp or cotton, can be chemically treated to produce either rayon or acetate filaments. Rayon is the tougher of the two, but acetate is more springy and elastic. Both can boast of a number of good attributes: they are non-wrinkling, moth and mildew proof, nonallergenic, washable, spot-resistant, and flexible. They may be spun into many sizes, textures, and weights, a quality which makes them valuable for copying or blending with natural fibers.

Acrylic. This fiber is soft, weather resistant, and warm. Easy to dye, acrylic does shrink in hot water.

Saran. A strong, clear plastic material, made from vinyl chloride, saran resists moisture and wear.

Nylon. A petroleum product, nylon is elastic and long wearing but can become brittle from too much light.

Orlon. This material is an acrylic resin product. Though light and fluffy, it is quite strong and takes weather and wear very well.

Polyester. Produced from tree resin, polyester blends well and is resistant to moisture, mildew, and wrinkling.

WEAVING DESIGN

Design in weaving results from a pleasing combination of fiber textures, color relationships, and form (or pattern). This gives weavers an enormous range of characteristics from which to construct a weaving; however, it also requires them to exercise a great deal of discrimination. Since most good design is based on a simple, direct approach, the weaver should think in terms of limiting this ocean of choices. Start with basic texture/color/form relationships and work gradually toward more complex design ideas. This will give you an opportunity to explore new ideas without being overwhelmed by your tools.

One very elementary aspect of design is to select materials whose characteristics best suit the function of the finished woven piece. This particularly applies to your choice of warp yarn. Any yarn selected for use in a warp must be strong because it undergoes a great deal of friction, stress, and stretching. Broken warp threads are a nuisance that can be avoided by first testing a prospective warp material. Take a single thread about a yard long between your hands and give it a few short, sharp tugs. If it snaps, it's probably not suitable.

Two methods can be used for choosing warp textures and colors: 1) Patterns may first be worked out on graph paper with colored pencils. Then warp and weft color arrangements are approximated and changed or otherwise adjusted until they mix properly. 2) Warp sequences may be planned by wrapping colored yarns around a yardstick at the correct number of ends to the inch. The sequence can be easily changed and variations worked out using the actual colors under consideration.

Patterns and colors can also be tested out on cardboard or nail looms ahead of time. To do this, weave small swatches set with the correct number of ends to the inch, employing the yarns to be used. This will help determine if the warp or the weft will dominate in the pattern.

Weft materials, unlike warp yarns, can range widely in strength—from uncombed lamb's fleece to highly spun plastic filaments. Since it isn't under tension while being used, almost anything can qualify as weft.

Think about the relationship of certain techniques to the function you are planning for a project. A satisfactory result will more than justify the time spent on drafting and design.

Here are some design approaches to consider. You may find a whole field of ideas in just one of these suggestions, but try to push on and think about all of them.

• Realize that the spacing of both warp and weft have a lot to do with the weight, feel, function, and final appearance of any fabric.
• Use pattern wisely—too much or too little will ruin a project.
• Repeats are tools that will help to balance all elements in a weaving. Shapes, colors, pattern, and plain areas can be used effectively more than once.
• Don't be carried away by fancy yarns or hundreds of colors; think of the basic form first of all. This includes finding inspiration in three-dimensional structures, natural and man-made, rather than just in color.
• Keep a focal point somewhere in the work. Use everything else to lead the eye into this center of attention.
• Create rhythm by relating the elements in your weav-

ing in such a way that eye movement is encouraged.

• Symmetrical designs will tend to have a formal, calm appearance, whereas movement and informality are the results of asymmetrical, or unbalanced, design.

• Interest can be maintained by keeping the number of elements or parts of any work uneven. Two units might be static; three are likely to cause visual movement throughout the work. This will draw the viewer's attention into a weaving, subtly evoking his appreciation of the design.

• Relate colors to one another and disregard texture. Then do the opposite.

• Try similar contrasts in form, in color, in texture.

• Finally—and most important—relate all parts of your work to each other so that a unified effect is achieved. Having everything working together will create much more excitement than having the work pulled apart by discordant elements.

As to creativity and originality, every individual has some, no matter how well hidden it may appear to be. Don't be discouraged if at first you have difficulty coming up with ideas or translating them into finished pieces. Each successive attempt will be more fluid and inventive. Don't give up. Interpret the things around you in terms of your own ideas. Really observe. Look at nature particularly, for there you can find color, form, and texture in perfect balance with one another. Architecture, industrial design, and other man-made objects, including art, are endless sources for ideas. Take time to become aware of the unending stimuli present in the world. It will be worthwhile both for your weavings and for you.

COLOR IN WEAVING

In any weaving employing more than one color, the mixture of hues, tones, and shading is probably the first characteristic the viewer notices. The closer one looks at a weaving, however, the more these large color areas begin to separate into points of pure hue which visually combine to make that area. Unlike paintings in which pleasing colors are combined by mixing pigments and balancing areas of solid color against one another, woven warp and weft colors intertwine to form optical mixtures; that is, the eye perceives a blending of two or more colors into one, though actually the colors are separate.

Yarn sizes and textures will also affect the final woven color. Instead of just putting two large masses of yarn together to decide if the colors relate well, take one strand of each and twist them around one another. This approximates their appearance when interwoven, giving a more accurate preview of the blend.

To understand color as an interrelating weaving element, take a look at the fiber color wheel on page 38. The outer circle contains pure hues which are the basic colors of the color wheel. This includes primary (red, blue, yellow), secondary (violet, orange, green), and tertiary colors (adjacent mixtures of color, such as blue-green or yellow-green).

Each hue has two other qualities: chroma, or a scale of the intensity of the color; and value, the placement of the color on a white to black scale. If you were to include 10 steps in each of these scales and 12 pure hues in the color wheel, there would be 1200 separate colors available to you. In reality there are many more. The middle circle of the color wheel shows the result of juxtapositioning opposites, or complementary colors, and the inner circle combines the complementaries.

Woven mixtures of color depend greatly on how much of any one color is used. There's a great deal of difference between a weave in which two colors are equally balanced and a pattern weave that divides these colors into definite unbalanced areas. Shades not even present can be suggested by beating one area of the weft more tightly than another. Consider these factors ahead of time; otherwise, what might appear to be a good color combination at first glance could turn out to be a rather poor one.

Remember that any single color is neither ugly nor beautiful. When properly balanced against one another or blended in just the right proportions, almost any color combination can be pleasing. Keep an open mind; don't let your preconceived notions of a color hold you back.

Some rules of thumb concerning how colors work with one another can be a good starting point:

• Complementary colors (those across the color wheel from one another) when placed next to each other will appear to be intensified and may even vibrate. However, when mixed, they produce a color with a dull grey cast.

• A single color area will have much greater depth and richness if it is made up of yarns in several shades of the same hue.

• When bright and neutral areas are contrasted, each brings out the essence of the other.

• It is often wise to use neutral tones to bind two opposing saturated hues.

• Neutrals themselves have shades. Off-white can have a pink, blue, brown, grey, green, or yellow cast.

A few more thoughts in regard to weaving colors:

• Whenever possible, relate the colors used in a weaving to the colors present in the area where it will ultimately be displayed or used.

• Warp color will affect the tone of the weft; that is, white warp dilutes weft colors, whereas a black warp intensifies and adds sparkle.

• Change yarn textures and shades within one hue for surface interest.

• A subtle appearance results from gradual change rather than by strong contrasts. On the other hand—though it is more difficult to master—contrast produces a lively surface.

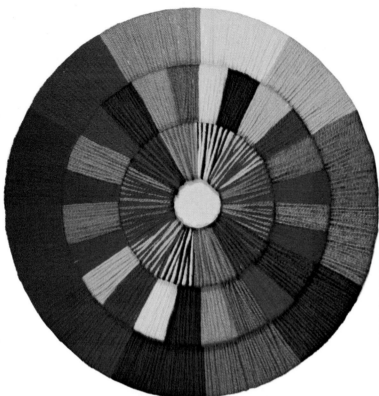

COLOR WHEEL *(left)* gives a visual idea of the inter-relation of yarn colors. The outer circle shows pure hues of the basic primary, secondary, and tertiary colors; the middle circle shows complementaries placed adjacent to one another; and the center circle has complementaries intermingled, approximating the effect of interwoven color.

UNUSUAL EFFECTS *are possible when you dye your own yarns* **(left to right):** *one color tie-dyed cotton warp, complementary colors overdyed at center, shades of one color, pure color over white yarn, blue and yellow overdyed at* center to make green, pure color over grey yarn, unifying two separate colors by overdyeing at the center, and a two color tie-dyed cotton warp. These are just a few of the many color variations available to you in home dyed yarns.

DYEING YARNS IN YOUR HOME

At times you will search for a particular color in a certain type of fiber but won't be able to find it. Don't be discouraged; turn this problem into a new, exciting experience by coloring your own yarns. Dyeing is a way to individualize your weaving materials through the use of commercial or natural dyestuffs.

Like gourmet cooking, the secret of achieving beautiful results depends on timing, proper ingredients mixed in proper proportions, and a good dye recipe. Books are available that are stocked with color recipes, especially those concerning natural dyes. These recipes are a great aid to the dyer, who can rely on them for specific information regarding any particular color or dye material.

Commercial dyes

By far the most readily available coloring agents, commercial dyes are usually stocked by dimestores, supermarkets, craft centers, or yarn and weaving supply stores in amounts that will dye one-half to one pound of yarn.

Because different materials require different dyes, be sure to check the label before you buy. Fiber-reactive dyes form a permanent chemical bond with cotton, linen, or silk; direct dyes that bond physically, not chemically, with fibers, work on cotton, linen, and viscose rayon; acid dyes, similar in effect to direct dyes, affect silk and wool; and household dyes, the least permanent of all, are used for most natural and synthetic fibers.

All of these dyes must be combined with either un-iodized salt or acetic acid (commonly available in the form of vinegar) in order to penetrate and dye fibers. Salt is used for everything except silk and wool, which require acetic acid. Frequently, household dyes will already contain salt, so be sure to read the label.

Methods vary according to dye type, but the initial step in dyeing yarns applies to all of them: any yarn to be dyed must first be wound into skeins and tied loosely, submerged in warm, soapy water (use soap flakes, not detergents) for about one hour, rinsed well, squeezed to remove excess water, then placed in the dye bath. Just remember that yarn looks darker when wet, so remove it when it is one shade darker than desired.

Dyestuff packages usually include all necessary information regarding the proper procedure to follow. Don't forget to wear old clothes or an apron. Do keep notes on time, temperature, and amounts used; it will then be easy to duplicate your efforts at a later date.

Natural dyes

To color yarns with a richness and subtlety unmatched by any other method, use natural dyes. These are collected from locally available plants or purchased from sources that import natural dyestuffs of other countries. Anything from the roots to the seeds of a plant may be used if they have a dye-producing quality; this includes such familiar plant products as onion skins, coffee beans, saffron, and walnut hulls.

Many dye-producing plants exist around your area. With your dye book in hand, check with local plant nurseries. You'll soon have a working knowledge of dye plants in your locale. Gather dyestuffs when they are in season and use immediately. If this isn't possible, store the cleaned dyestuff in the freezer.

There are two steps to natural dyeing: mordanting and applying the dyestuff. The mordant is a chemical salt that opens the fibers so they can bite (from *mordere*, a Latin verb meaning to bite) onto the dye. Because of this process, natural dyes are fixed into the yarn and are usually extremely colorfast.

Some local dyes and a number of imported ones are sold by many weaving supply stores, often by mail order. Some places also sell mordants, which can be ordered from chemical supply companies, as well.

Yarns are prepared for natural dyeing in the same way that they are readied for commercial dyes, except that they are first boiled in the mordant, then allowed to rest for a day or more. Meanwhile, the dyestuff is usually steeped overnight and boiled for several hours.

When everything is ready, the dyestuff goes into a large stainless steel or enamel pot with plenty of water —enough to cover the yarn. Once mordanted, the yarn is submerged in the dyebath, and the mixture is slowly brought to a boil or simmer. The dyebath should be gently stirred to assure that dye penetrates all surfaces of the yarn.

After the yarn has been simmered for the correct amount of time, the stove is turned off, but the yarn sits in the dyebath until cool. If earlier removal is necessary, the yarn should be rinsed in successive baths from hot to cool. Finally, the yarn is hung in the shade to dry.

Dyes can alter the existing color of a yarn or even produce stunning, unusual effects. With some of the following applications you can expand your interest as well as your results.

- White yarn gives a pure color but grey or beige yarn yield beautifully softened colors.
- Try overdyeing on one yarn in two or more colors.
- You can graduate shades by dipping one portion of the yarn into one color, another into a second shade.
- To tone down a strong color, overdye it in a weak dyebath of its complementary color.
- To deepen or lighten any tone, either dye it with the same color in a deeper tone or bleach it.

Learning to use dyes effectively gives a new dimension to many weaving techniques and can add vastly to the scope of your woven work. For some examples of dye applications you can do at home, see the color photo on the opposite page.

Weaving Techniques and Projects

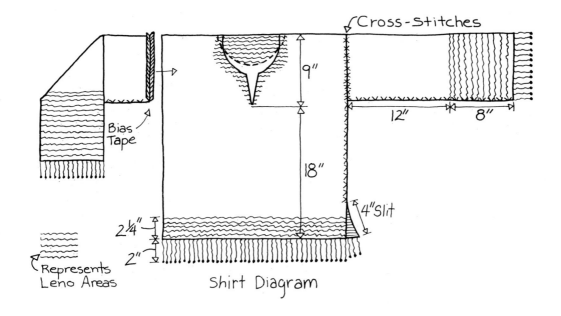

Cross-Stitches

9"

Bias Tape

18"

12"   8"

4" Slit

2¼"

2"

Represents Leno Areas

Shirt Diagram

The term *weaving* covers a lot of ground. Its meaning can range from tapestry work to basketmaking with stops along the way for Swedish pattern weaves, rya rug knotting, lace weaves, or painted warp work. And yet these are just a sampling of its many, *many* applications and uses.

The projects and techniques on the following pages should whet your appetite for weaving—they are really the first stepping stones on the path towards gaining an appreciation for and understanding of the craft. Ideas for woven articles vary from purely functional to purely decorative, yet all are enhanced by the planned use of the special techniques described and illustrated on these pages. If finished in different ways, some of the projects have more than one possible use. All are shown in full color, as are selected examples of the same or related techniques used by advanced and professional weavers. These examples should give you an idea of how simple methods can be worked

into unique statements of style and personal vision.

Preliminary information on looms and how to use them are discussed on the previous pages, which should be read by the beginner before attempting to undertake these projects. Measurements, amounts, and tools required are given for floor looms as well as frame or table looms, and instructions are geared to apply to all looms suggested for any given project.

There is a lot to think about when you are preparing a project for weaving. A few pointers and suggestions will help things to go smoothly:

Read *all* measurements, amounts, equipment listed, and instructions before buying anything or beginning your weaving preparations. This will prevent any oversight or misunderstanding from cropping up later when you are well into your work.

Use the weaving drafts given in graph form with each project as a guide to threading your loom. Instead

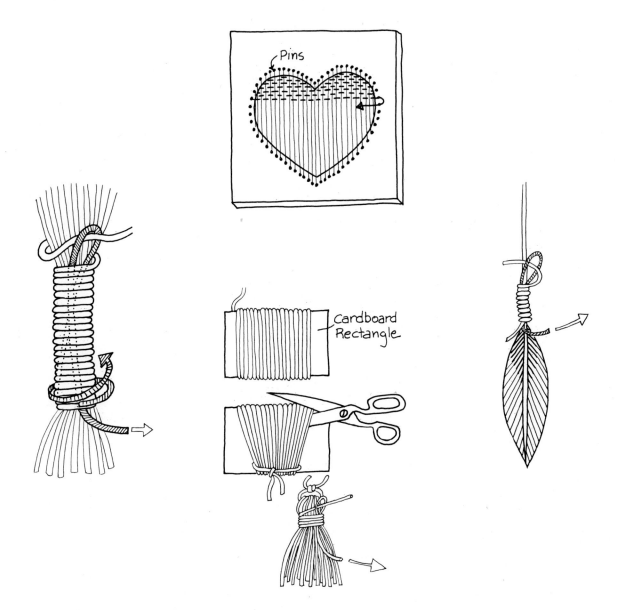

of trying to read treadling information directly from the graph, translate it into written form and use it this way when weaving. Things will go more quickly with less chance of making mistakes.

The discrepancy between the measurements given for warping the loom and the measurements given for the finished piece exists because drawing in at the selvages during weaving or shrinkage when a piece is cleaned during finishing will alter the original size. Do not try to use the measurements given for the finished piece unless you are an experienced weaver.

Some designs given in this book are based on a grid, or graph, system which can be used to enlarge the design to any size. To find the actual size of the design, note the equivalent measurement given for one square of the grid (example: ⅝-inch equals 1 inch, or 1 square equals 1 inch by 1 inch). Add up the number of squares in the *actual size* across and lengthwise to get the width and height. Draw an outline of

this size and then divide it into the same number of squares across and down as exist in the original graph. When finished, you will have a larger rectangle subdivided into squares which corresponds to the original graph. Now break down the design into square units and transfer these units to the actual size graph square by square.

As you look at the projects and special examples shown on the color pages, new ideas for your own projects will certainly arise. Feel free to interpret our project ideas in other colors, other yarns . . . even in other techniques. Just remember to make adjustments for your changes in the amounts and measurements listed. For information on yarn estimation refer to pages 32 and 33. Try the various techniques on different woven articles to create your own personal look, and if you so desire, convert our ideas into projects that work for you. In short, the information and ideas given on these pages are raw materials for your creativity.

Tapestry: What It Is

Tapestry is really the art of joining together rows or sections of woven color to create a design. Butterfly or tapestry bobbins are used instead of shuttles to carry many different weft colors, and strong, widely spaced warp ends (usually set at 6 to 8 per inch) provide a framework on which these weft yarns are woven in plain weave and beaten down to completely cover the warp. The spacing or *sett* of the warp ends forms a rib-like appearance on the surface of the cloth. Tapestries are traditionally woven so that the ribs will run horizontally rather than vertically when completed; that is, the tapestry is turned on its side when taken from the loom and mounted for display. Since there are many weft picks to the inch, the weft itself is stronger and more supportive than the warp.

Of all weaving techniques, tapestry is one of the easiest to learn. When you have developed a mastery of its methods of construction, an understanding of other weaving techniques can follow naturally.

One of the oldest weaving methods in existence, tapestry has ranged from fine Egyptian and Peruvian works through Medieval pictorial weavings to the present-day variety of styles. Two schools of thought exist concerning tapestry: the traditional, where technique is a tool subordinated to a previously conceived flat surface design; and the modern, where texture and technique combine with color and shading in the construction of free-form tapestry works. Traditional examples are displayed on pages 4 and 5; for more current interpretations, note the pieces shown on page 46.

Simplicity of design and a limited color palette are keys to a successful tapestry. A basic color selection of just 15 colors can be expanded to more than 675 by blending colors, running color areas into one another, and mixing grey, white, or black with any single shade. A limited range provides good over-all color blending without diluting the visual impact.

The actual weaving of a tapestry may be done on a simple stretcher-frame nail loom, as well as on upright looms and floor looms. Short strands of tapestry weft may be needlewoven, or butterfly bobbins or small balls of the weft yarn can be used. In any kind of complex tapestry work, however, tapestry bobbins are very helpful. In all cases a comb-like beater or the tip of the bobbin is used to pack the weft.

Warp materials must be very strong to withstand the frequent beating and tight tension required for tapestry work. The yarn should be tightly spun with a smooth surface; smooth linen, Navajo wool rug warp, cotton carpet warp, or a strong cotton twine are possibilities.

Weft yarns should be materials with some tooth and body, yet soft enough to completely cover the warp when beaten down tightly. Slippery or delicate yarns are really not suitable; the best weft materials are wool, silk, soft cotton, or any synthetic yarn with similar properties. Needlepoint wool yarn is very good; metal threads are occasionally used to add sparkle.

The design for a tapestry is usually worked out to scale on graph paper. The proposed piece is drawn in outline and the design and colors are selected. The scale drawing is next enlarged to actual size. This can be done by projecting a slide of the design onto a wall, adjusting the size to fit, and taking a tracing onto heavy paper or bleached muslin. This is called a cartoon and serves as a working pattern and color guide when fastened to the tapestry frame *behind* the warp. On a frame loom, the cartoon is taped to the back of the loom and left in place until the weaving is finished. When an upright or a floor loom will be used, the cartoon is taped to the apron rod or pinned to the woven heading and unrolled as the weaving progresses. The unwoven portion of the cartoon can be supported by a bar attached to the body of the loom below the harness section. As the weaving progresses, the design and tapestry are rolled on together.

A critical problem in tapestry weaving is the tendency for selvages to draw in due to the combination of strong warp tension and changes in the sizes of color areas across the warp. Prevention includes doubling the selvage warp ends, lashing the edges of the tapestry to the frame of the loom as the work progresses (for simple looms only), or using a rug temple or brace across the warp to hold the woven edges rigid. This is an expandable tool with teeth at either end that grab the selvages and keep them at the proper width.

The methods used for joining or blending color areas in tapestry are given in diagrams on pages 44 and 45. They include interlocking weft, overlapping joins and dovetailing, all used for joining adjacent color areas; vertical slit and diagonal slit for open tapestry slits and joining vertical or diagonal color areas; and hatching, which is used when gradual shading from one color to another is desired.

When a tapestry is completed, remove it from the loom and knot off the warp ends in pairs or groups to secure the last row of the weft. If no fringe is desired, add an extra 3 to 4 inches of plain weave at each end, edge with carpet tape, fold under, and whipstitch to the back of the piece. Dowels or rods may be sewn to the carpet tape for hanging purposes, or two lengths of curved molding can be screwed together and clamped over the top edge.

*TAPESTRY SAMPLER **(at right)** is a good way to learn simple tapestry technique. Directions begin on page 45. "Sunshine and Shadows" **(below, left)** is a literal landscape with tapestry-like appearance, enlivened by variations in yarn texture and the addition of twill weave, soumak knotting, and 50-50 tabby, in which warp and weft are of equal weight. Rep rug **(below, right)** combines shades of mauve, cornflower blue, and white in selvage to selvage weave patterns formed by alternating the colors used in simple 4-harness pattern variations.*

DESIGN: MARI SPEYER

DESIGN: SYLVIA LOVELL-COOPER

DESIGN: MARY HEWLETT

A Tapestry Sampler

(Color photo on page 43, top)

Making a sampler will introduce you to the various techniques employed in tapestry work. The sampler shown on page 43 uses interlocking weft, dovetail joins, vertical slit, diagonal slit, and hatching—as well as vertical stripe and spaced dot weft patterns—in its construction. This sampler uses a warp material that has been integrated into the visual design of the sampler. Should you want a more traditional appearance, use the alternate warp material indicated below and beat the weft more firmly to completely cover warp. Leave weft tails hanging at back of tapestry.

Equipment: Stretcher Bar Frame Loom, 4-Harness Frame Loom, or Floor Loom; scissors, tape measure, comb beater, and tapestry needle, or bobbins.

Final size: 12½ inches by 15 inches.
Warp: 4 ounces black 3 ply tapestry yarn set 13 inches wide at 6 ends to the inch. (Alternate warp material: 1 roll 4 ply black cotton carpet warp set 13 inches wide at 6 ends to the inch.)
Warp length: Stretcher Bar Loom: 20 inches; 4-Harness Frame Loom: 72 inches; Floor Loom: 1½ yards.
Weft: 3 strand Mexican handspun wool tapestry yarn in the following colors and amounts: dark green, 1 ounce; medium green, 1 ounce; light green, 1 ounce; grey green, ½-ounce; navy blue, 1 ounce; medium blue, 1 ounce; sky blue, 1 ounce; grey blue, 1½ ounce; and pale blue, 1 ounce. Picks per inch: 8 to 18, depending on design.

Weaving pattern: Plain Weave (see graph 44-A below).
Finishing: Twining and hemming.

HOW TO MAKE

Follow diagram on facing page for all measurements and as a key to techniques used in specific areas.
1. Twine warp ends into place with dark green yarn (drawing 44-B below), then weave 4 rows of dark green.
2. Vertical Stripes: alternate two weft colors in every other row. Example: blue, green, blue, green; repeat.
3. Offset Vertical Stripes: weave as explained in step 2 until the line of change is reached. Then weave two successive rows of the same color before returning to the alternating color plan for stripes.
4. Vertical Slit: begin both wefts at edge away from slit. Weave the two colors towards one another until they meet at the place where a slit is desired. At this point, they will each circle *adjacent* warp ends. The shed is then changed and the two colors return to their starting points. The vertical opening is formed because the two weft colors *do not* circle the same warp end or each other (drawing 44-C).
5. Working on more than two adjacent color areas: any number of color areas may be woven simultaneously, with either overlapping joins (drawing 44-D) or

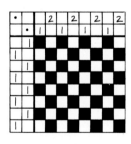

44 -A Plain Weave

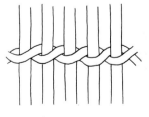

44 -B Twining

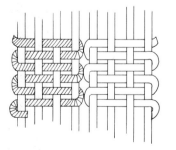

44-C Vertical Slit

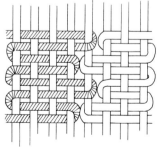

44-D Overlapping Joins

vertical or diagonal slits between them. Always have the weft yarns approaching or withdrawing from one another; never have them all moving in the same direction at once.

6. Diagonal Slits: two weft colors approach and return from one another as with the vertical slit, but instead of turning at the same point in succeeding weft passes, the turning point moves *one or more* warp ends *to the right* or *to the left* of the previous turn (drawing 45-A). Curved diagonal slits are made in much the same way. Two or more matching successive turns (depending on the shape of the curve) are worked before moving over one or more warp ends. When weaving curves, it is best to follow a cartoon.

7. Hatching: two weft yarns approach, meet, and return from one another in a series of joins which meet first inside of one color area, then well into the second color area in a random overlapping fashion. The overlap creates the appearance of a third color in the overlapping ground (drawing 45-B).

8. Dovetail Interlock: two adjacent color weft yarns approach, meet, and turn, circling a common warp end as a turning point (drawing 45-C).

9. Interlocking Weft: two adjacent weft yarns approach, meet, and circle around one another before returning to their starting points (drawing 45-D).

Finishing. At the upper edge, twine warp ends into place with navy weft yarn. Remove sampler from loom and press lightly with a steam iron to flatten. Turn all fringe to the back of the piece and whipstitch into place. To display your piece, hang it from a dowel or branch.

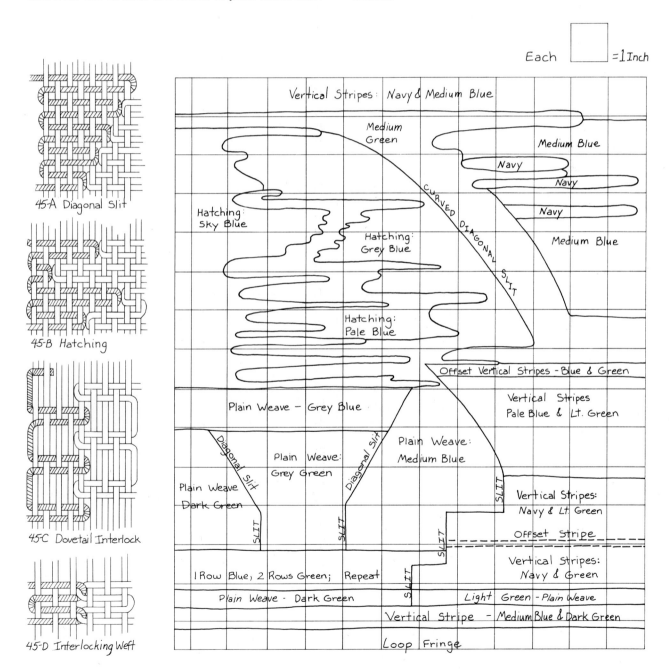

Each ☐ =1 Inch

45-A Diagonal Slit

45-B Hatching

45-C Dovetail Interlock

45-D Interlocking Weft

Vertical Stripes: Navy & Medium Blue

Medium Green

Medium Blue

Navy

Navy

Navy

Medium Blue

Hatching: Sky Blue

Hatching: Grey Blue

CURVED DIAGONAL SLIT

Hatching: Pale Blue

Offset Vertical Stripes - Blue & Green

Plain Weave - Grey Blue

Vertical Stripes Pale Blue & Lt. Green

Plain Weave: Medium Blue

Diagonal Slit

Plain Weave: Grey Green

Diagonal Slit

SLIT

Plain Weave Dark Green

Vertical Stripes: Navy & Lt. Green

SLIT

Offset Stripe

Vertical Stripes: Navy & Green

SLIT

1 Row Blue, 2 Rows Green; Repeat

Plain Weave - Dark Green

Light Green - Plain Weave

Vertical Stripe - Medium Blue & Dark Green

Loop Fringe

DESIGN: SACHI HONMYO

TAPESTRY can take on a new look when it is stitched and padded. Directions for quilted hanging *(right)* begin on the facing page. "Rain Washes Roots Free" *(below, left)* is a tour de force of subtle coloration. Mauve, earth tones, and greys in plain and twill weave variations are convincingly blended through the selective use of tapestry joins. Overtones of Africa color this stylized portrait *(lower right)* executed in tapestry, rya, and rep weaves.

DESIGN: MARY BALZER BUSKIRK

DESIGN: NANCY LAWTON

Quilted Tapestry Hanging

(Color photo on facing page, top)

Variations in its color and texture, as well as machine quilting, give a rich appearance to this diminutive but striking wall hanging. Seen on our cover as well, its bold design makes it the perfect choice for adding eye appeal to any small wall area.

Equipment: 2-Harness Frame Loom (see page 10 for directions): comb beater, 9-inch by 12-inch rectangles of plain muslin and cotton print for lining and backing, loose dacron batt, sewing machine or needle, orange-red thread, and a 12-inch long red enameled half-round dowel.

Finished size: 8 inches by 11 inches.
Warp: 31 yards of 4 ply grape colored heavy cotton warp set 8 inches wide at 10 ends to the inch.
Weft: An assortment of yarns in a variety of textures (Mexican handspun, tapestry wool, serape wool, embroidery floss, rattail, and suede strips) and colors, as shown in the color key list below. These yarns are all ends from previously purchased yarn. If you have other colors that you have collected, use them instead —very small amounts are needed.
Weaving pattern: Plain Weave (drawing 47-A).
Finishing: Seaming, quilting, and backing.

HOW TO MAKE

1. Enlarge the design on page 48 to the proper size and make a weaving cartoon as described on page 42.
2. Weave 3 inches of heading, then begin tapestry work according to the color keyed diagram on page 48, using the techniques shown in diagrams 44-D and 45-A through 45-D as needed.
3. When the arches are completed, weave 1½ inches more in red tones, then add 2½ inches in horizontal orange and grape ice stripes. This will later be folded over and used as a channel for carrying the dowel.
4. Remove weaving from the loom and unravel all but 1 inch of heading. Knot off fringe to secure the edges and trim to 1 inch.

Finishing. Place the weaving face *up* over the muslin rectangle and pin together firmly. Using red-orange thread, sew through both layers, along the outlines of each arch, the central rectangle, and the purple stripe along the bottom edge. *Do not sew* across the *bottoms* of the arches, rectangle, or the *ends* of the purple stripe. These areas *must* be kept open (see 47-B).

Tear off small bits of batting and push it into the channels formed by sewing between each colored arch with a wooden dowel. When the arches, rectangles, and purple stripe are stuffed, sew across the openings used to stuff these sections and trim the muslin to ¼-inch from the stitching line; remove all pins. Lay the rectangle of printed cotton face *up* on a flat surface, then place the padded weaving face *down* over the cotton and pin together. Seam both layers together along the sides and bottom, going under the stuffed purple stripe.

Leave 3 inches of weaving free on the upper edge, trim all corners, turn the piece to the right side, and fold under the free edge of the cotton fabric. Slip the upper edge of the weaving under the edge of the cotton to make a ¾-inch wide channel for the dowel. Whipstitch the weaving and fabric (drawing 47-C) and insert dowel.

47-A Plain Weave

47-B Keep Channels Open

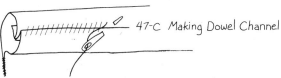
47-C Making Dowel Channel

Diagram Color Key

1. Deep Purple	7. Mexican Red	13. Deep Pink
2. Suede Purple	8. Dusty Red	14. Grape Ice
3. Magenta	9. Red Orange	15. Orange
4. Deep Violet	10. Pale Rust	16. Bright Orange
5. Hot Pink	11. Rust	17. Yellow Orange
6. Pale Violet	12. Indian Red	18. Black

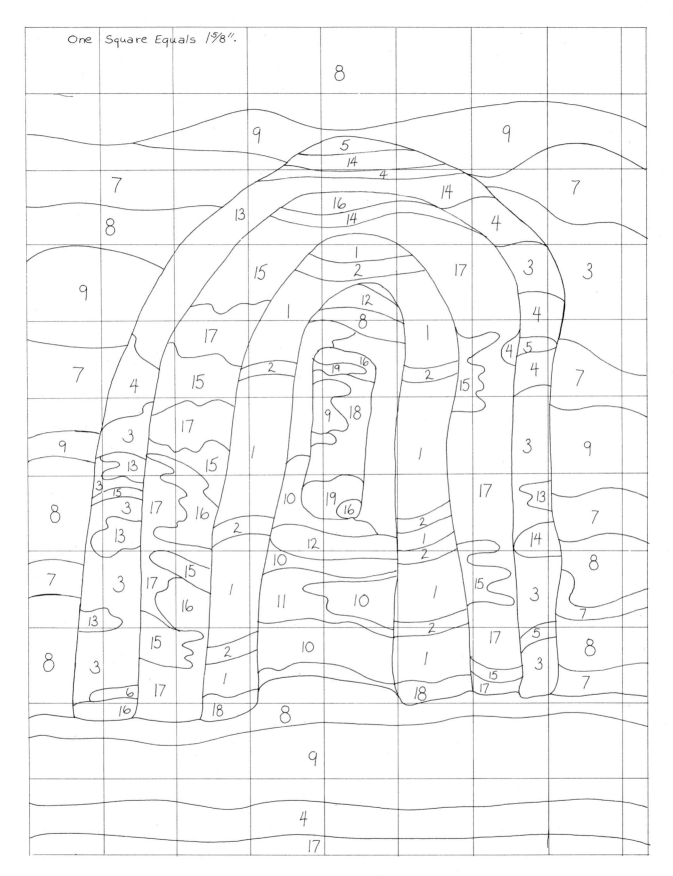

Diagram for Quilted Hanging

The Rya Rug

(Color photo on page 51, top)

Though most commonly applied in a traditional manner, the rya technique lends itself to other interesting effects. This fleece-like wool, roving, and novelty yarn creation is a good example. It consists of an off-white central design splashed with a vivid spot of color and flanked by a rich, chocolate-brown "sheepskin." The central portion is made in one piece; six smaller rectangular sections constitute the sheepskin area.

Rya knot technique. A member of the pile-woven rug family (which includes Oriental and flossa rugs), the rya has its traditional roots in Scandinavia where it was originally used for protection against winter cold.

The technique for rya pile consists of hand-knotting individual yarn tufts across the warp in rows which are separated by several picks of tabby weave. The number of tabby rows between knotted rows, the number of knots per inch, and the length of the yarn tufts all determine the density and lie of the pile. Warp ends are usually set at 6 to 8 per inch with doubled warp ends at the selvages for strength. Rya knots (also called ghiordes knots) vary from 2 to 4 per inch. Tabby weave is used at the start and the finish of the rug to reinforce the ends.

Rya rug designs are worked out to scale on graph paper, showing the relative size of the rug and the number of knots to the square inch. Sketches in crayon or pastel determine color placement.

Figuring the amount of yarn needed for the rya knots is not difficult. Simply multiply the desired length of the pile by two and add ½-inch. The result is multiplied by the number of knots in one row and how many strands are contained in a knot; this amount is next multiplied by the number of knotted rows in the rug. The resulting number will give the total inches of yarn needed. Divide by 36 for total yardage. Warp and background weft amounts are figured as for most woven pieces (see pages 32 and 33).

The rya knot itself can be made in two ways: 1) precut rya lengths are made by wrapping yarn around a cardboard rectangle of the correct size and then cutting across one edge (drawing 49-A). These lengths are then knotted individually or in groups onto the warp by pulling each end of cut length around, under, and up through a pair of adjacent warp ends (drawing 49-B). 2) A yardstick or slat is placed across the closed warp and a continuous length of yarn is looped around the warp and around the slat in a specific pattern, giving a single, uniform pile length across the warp (drawing 49-C). To make pile, cut loops and remove stick.

Often, more than one strand of yarn is included in a single knot, especially where shades or compliments of a single color are combined to add brilliance and variety to the pile. Any color has more depth and richness when formulated from a variety of shades. For comparison, think of the technique used by Seurat and other pointillist painters.

Equipment: 4-Harness Frame Loom: stick shuttle, slat or comb beater, cardboard rectangle, scissors, tape measure. Floor Loom: stick shuttle, cardboard rectangle, scissors, tape measure.

Finished size: Six dark rectangles: each 9 inches by 14 inches; 1 off-white square: 20 inches by 20 inches. Combined size: approx. 58 inches by 28 inches.

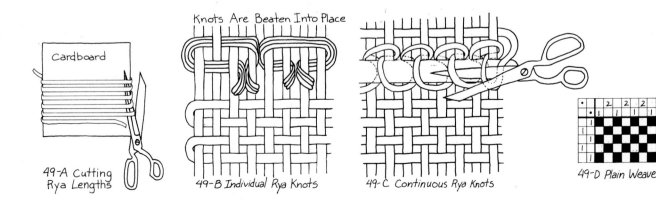

49-A Cutting Rya Lengths

Knots Are Beaten Into Place
49-B Individual Rya Knots

49-C Continuous Rya Knots

49-D Plain Weave

Warp: 6 dark rectangles: 10 ounces of charcoal grey 3 ply heavy carpet wool set 10 inches wide at 7 ends to the inch. Off-white square: 8 ounces oatmeal 3 ply carpet wool set 21 inches wide, 7 ends per inch.

Warp length: 4-Harness Frame Loom: dark rectangles, 72 inches (make two consecutive warps having 3 rug sections per warp); off-white square, 54 inches. Floor Loom: dark rectangles, 4 yards; white square, 2 yards.

Weft: Tabby Rows: for 6 dark rectangles, 10 ounces charcoal grey 3 ply heavy carpet wool; for off-white square, 8 ounces oatmeal 3 ply heavy carpet wool. Picks per inch: 7 to 8. Rya Knots: dark rectangles: 2 pounds thin horsehair yarn, 3¼ pounds heavy horsehair yarn, both in dark brown tones; 1 pound uncombed unspun brown/black fleece; 2½ pounds South American handspun one ply wool in brown and caramel; 1 pound 3 ounces one ply Mexican handspun wool in dark brown. Off-white square: 2 ounces unspun natural colored flax; 8 ounces *each* of white cotton chenille, ecru rayon bouclé, cream/caramel slub rayon/linen 2 ply, and 4 ply cream-colored shiny rayon; 2¼ pounds cream colored South American handspun one ply wool; 1 pound 3 ounces one ply Mexican handspun wool in off-white; 12 ounces cream colored wool roving rope; one ounce *each* purple, magenta, orange 3 ply carpet wool. Knotted rows per inch: 1.

Weaving pattern: Plain Weave (see graph 49-D).

Finishing: Twining, knotted fringe, selvage joins.

HOW TO MAKE

Dark rectangles.

1. Twine warp ends into place, then make a 2-inch heading followed by 2 inches of tabby weave.

2. Tie 1 row of rya knots, each secured over 4 warp ends and containing four to six pre-cut 10- to 12-inch strands of heavy horsehair, thin horsehair, unspun brown fleece, South American brown and caramel handspun, and brown Mexican handspun wool (vary the contents of each knot for a random surface appearance). Knot selvages as shown in drawing 49-B.

3. Begin the next inch of plain weave, making sure that the first shed to be opened is not the same as the last shed before the finished row of rya knots.

4. Repeat steps 2 and 3 until 11 rows of rya knots have been woven, then weave 2 final inches of tabby weave. Leave 4 inches for finishing before going on to the next rectangle. Repeat steps 1 through 4 for each rectangle.

Off-white square

Follow steps 1 through 4 as for dark rectangles, with the following exceptions: use cotton chenille, rayon boucle, slub rayon/linen, cream colored South American handspun, and off-white Mexican handspun yarns for knots, following the diagram below as a key to placement of colors and textures for shiny rayon, unspun flax, wool rope, and colored carpet wools, as well as the materials previously mentioned; also, complete 16 rows of rya knots before weaving last 2 inches of tabby weave.

Finishing. Remove pieces from loom and take out headings. Tie off all fringe in pairs as shown in photo 25-C on page 25. Clip all fringe to 2 inches and, wrong side up, fold the 2 inch tabby weave strips back until the first row of knots appears. Whipstitch strips to back with heavy carpet thread. Join all pieces as shown in drawing 50-A below with heavy carpet warp and a tapestry needle. Use the technique shown on page 25, photo 25-B.

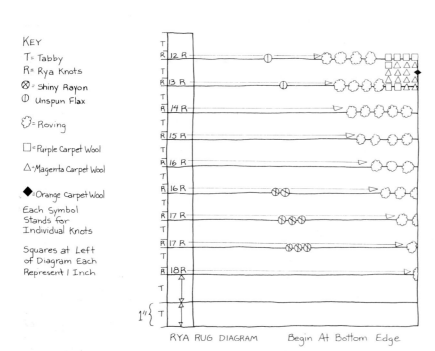

KEY
T = Tabby
R = Rya Knots
⊗ = Shiny Rayon
⓪ = Unspun Flax
✿ = Roving
□ = Purple Carpet Wool
△ = Magenta Carpet Wool
◆ = Orange Carpet Wool

Each Symbol Stands for Individual Knots

Squares at Left of Diagram Each Represent 1 Inch

RYA RUG DIAGRAM   Begin At Bottom Edge

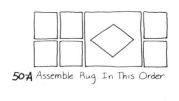

50-A Assemble Rug In This Order

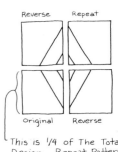

This is ¼ of The Total Design. Repeat Pattern Once and Reverse Twice, Then Combine For A Total Cartoon of Design.

DESIGN: DOCEY LEWIS

DESIGN: LESTER RHINEHART

RYA KNOTS produce more than one effect; the shaggy rug shown in the photo above resembles a sheepskin. Directions begin on page 49. "Hibiscus at the Royal Hawaiian" **(at left)** is a cascade of colorful mohair yarns rya knotted into widely separated horizontal rows. Rya rug **(lower right)** conforms to Scandinavian tradition of technique, yet captures the flavor of the Sierra in its colors.

DESIGN: ROSALIND WATKIN

Open Warp Shoulder Bag

(Color photo on page 54, top)

A fringe-trimmed shoulder bag is just the thing for casual wear, especially when it comes in bright, ice cream sherbet colors. The purse was woven sideways on the loom, then joined along its sides by tying the fringe together. A polished elkhorn button secures the flap.

Spaced warp technique. Used effectively for pillows, clothing, or curtains, spaced warp weaving allows for open areas in the body of the cloth. These are formed by grouping warp ends together, leaving spaces of varying widths between these groups. The piece is then woven evenly, making a length of cloth with open vertical spaces crossed by floating horizontal weft threads. (See drawing 52-A.)

Equipment: 4-Harness Frame Loom: stick shuttle, beater, scissors, tape measure, tapestry needle. Floor Loom: same as for Frame Loom. Other materials: 10-inch by 22-inch rectangle of yellow felt, needle, yellow thread, polished elkhorn button for closure.

Unfinished cloth: 8½ inches by 24 inches.
Finished purse: 8½ inches by 10 inches.
Warp: 75 yards *each* of orange mohair bouclé and coral 10/2 linen; 57 yards *each* of yellow rayon bouclé and coral 4-ply mercerized crochet cotton; and 38 yards of *each* of the following yarns: royal blue 10/2 linen, baby blue rayon bouclé, and turquoise 4-ply mercerized crochet cotton. These yarns are set 25 inches wide at 10 ends to the inch in the following color order.
Warp color order: (This is a 2-inch repeat.) Coral linen, yellow bouclé, turquoise crochet cotton, orange bouclé, coral linen, yellow bouclé, coral crochet cotton, orange bouclé, orange bouclé, yellow bouclé, coral crochet cotton, coral linen, baby blue bouclé, turquoise crochet cotton, coral crochet cotton, orange bouclé, coral linen, royal blue linen, royal blue linen, baby blue bouclé.

For warp spaces, group warp ends and leave spaces in the following order: 5 ends, ½-inch space; 30 ends, ¼-inch space; 27 ends, ½-inch space; 25 ends, ½-inch space; 15 ends, ¼-inch space; 17 ends, ½-inch space; 30 ends, ½-inch space; 17 ends, ¼-inch space; 25 ends, ½-inch space; 15 ends, ½-inch space; 10 ends.
Warp length: 4-Harness Frame Loom: 1½ yards. Floor Loom: 1½ yards.
Weft: 75 yards of coral 10/2 linen. Picks per inch: 14.
Weaving pattern: Plain Weave (see graph 52-B for threading, treadling, and tie-up).
Finishing: Fringe, lining, and hand-sewn button.

HOW TO MAKE

1. Weave 8 inches of heading for fringe, using heavy yarn or rag strips.
2. With 10/2 coral colored linen as weft, weave 3½ inches from selvage to selvage, keeping edges even and without loops.
3. At this point begin a tapestry slit at the left edge of the weaving, using the weft space that is 5 warp ends in from the selvage as the vertical slit area (drawing 52-C). Make a slit long enough to accommodate a large

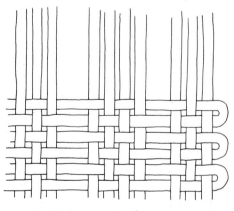

52-A Open Warp Appearance

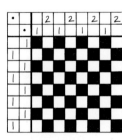

52 B Plain Weave

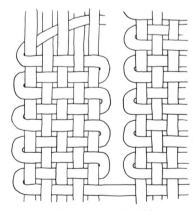

52-C Tapestry Slit

button (1½ inches is a good size), weaving the right hand side of the slit first, then the left-hand side.

4. When the slit is long enough, run the remaining linen to the opposite selvage, loop it around the last selvage thread, and run a 2-inch-long tail back into the open shed. Change sheds and beat into place.

5. Continue to weave for 3½ inches until the purse is the same width on either side of the tapestry slit. Then weave in 12 inches of rags or heavy yarn as a divider to allow for fringe.

6. At this point begin to weave again with the coral colored linen weft, and continue until a 2½-inch-wide strip for the purse strap is woven.

7. Remove the entire warp from the loom, unravelling all headings and dividers (heavy yarns or rag strips), then cut apart as shown in drawing 53-A, leaving 8 inches of fringe on either side of the purse and 4 inches on either side of the strap.

Finishing. Lay the purse body out flat with the right side down. Measure and mark the purse into two consecutive lengths of 10 inches *each*, followed by a 4-inch length (including the tapestry slit) for the purse flap. Fold the two 10-inch lengths together right sides out and secure the edges of the purse by knotting the purse back fringe to the purse front fringe (drawing 53-B). Continue to tie these purse edges together until all ends are secured. Next knot all fringe on the edges of the purse flap in pairs to prevent unraveling.

Measure the width and depth of the purse body, then cut the rectangle of yellow felt twice as long as the purse body, and the same width but minus ¼-inch. Fold the felt rectangle in half across the length and whipstitch the sides closed (drawing 53-C). This forms a felt liner, which is then inserted into the purse body and adjusted until it fits properly. Sew the liner to the purse body along the upper edges with a running stitch in coral linen matching the stitches to a similarly colored area on the outside of the purse.

Knot pairs of fringe on the purse strap to prevent unraveling; both ends of the strap should be tapered by gathering the weft together as tightly as possible when knotting for about the last inch. Pin one end of the finished strap to the inside of the purse, across the seam of the felt lining ½-inch from the top edge of the felt. Whipstitch into place (drawing 53-D). Repeat for second strap end.

To sew button closure in place, close flap of purse and mark with a safety pin where tapestry slit falls on purse front. Sew button into place with coral linen.

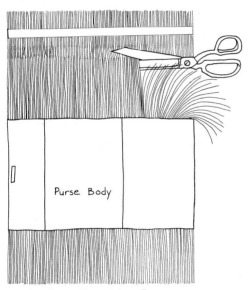

53-A Cutting Warp Fringe

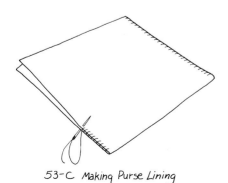

53-C Making Purse Lining

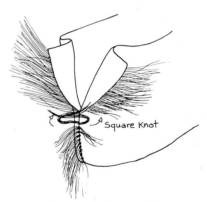

53-B Joining Purse Back to Front

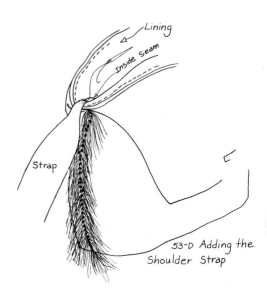

53-D Adding the Shoulder Strap

DESIGN: ALYSON SMITH GONSALVES

OPEN WARP allows lining to show through in this fringed shoulder bag **(at left).** Directions begin on page 52. Fringed tablerunner in satin weave makes a beautiful table decoration **(lower left);** or make yourself an elegant hostess skirt by splitting it into two equal lengths **(lower right).** Directions begin on the facing page.

DESIGN: MARI SPEYER

DESIGN: MARI SPEYER

Satin Weave Table Runner or Skirt

(Color photos on facing page, bottom left and right)

A skirt or a table runner—you can make either from this 84-inch length of satin weave warp-striped material. The full length may be finished with fringe and displayed as a runner on your dining table or buffet; or cut the length in half, line it, add an elasticized waistband, and you'll have a beautifully unique hostess skirt.

Satin weave technique. One of the three basic weave patterns, this method produces rich luxurious fabric with a smooth surface. The weave is based on a 5-thread warp sequence as shown on pages 8 and 9. The points at which the warp ends rise to the face of the cloth are spaced as far apart as possible to allow the weft threads to predominate. On the reverse side of the cloth, the warp threads are most visible.

A 5-thread sequence means that a fifth harness will have to be added to any 4-harness system you will be using. To do this, thread the loom with a 5-thread repeat, then tie heddles from harness one to the first thread in each repeat, from harness 2 to the second thread in each repeat, from harness 3 to the third thread, and from harness 4 to the fourth thread, leaving the fifth thread unattached. Then use a 3-inch-wide wooden slat that is 2 inches longer than the width of the loom to pick up every fifth thread across the warp (drawing 55-A). To form the fifth shed, slide the stick to a point directly behind the harnesses and then turn it up on edge.

Equipment: 4-Harness Table Loom: stick shuttle, beater, 3-inch-wide slat 2 inches longer than the width of the woven piece, scissors, tape measure. Floor Loom: stick shuttle, 3-inch-wide slat 2 inches longer than the width of the woven piece, scissors, tape measure. Additional materials: 2½ yards blue lining, 1 yard of ½-inch elastic, blue thread, needle or sewing machine.

Finished size: Table runner—22 inches by 84 inches. Skirt panels—each, 21 inches by 40 inches.

Warp: ⅛ pound *each* of navy blue, turquoise, dark green, lime green, and mustard gold 1 ply number 5 tightly spun Swedish worsted wool yarn set 23 inches wide at 10 ends per inch.

Warp color order: n—navy, t—turquoise, lg—light green, dg—dark green, m—mustard gold, x—repeat the sequence within those commas. 14 n, 8 t, 2 lg, 2 n, 2 t, 2 lg, 2 n, 2 m, 5 dg, 1 m and 1 dg x 3, 1 m, 6 t, 4 n, 4 lg, 1 dg, 1 m, 1 lg, 2 dg, 2 lg, 3 m, 3 dg, 2 n, 3 t, 2 lg, 3 n, 2 m, 2 n, 6 t, 2 dg, 2 lg, 3 t, 2 lg, 1 dg, 2 t, 2 dg, 2 lg, 8 dg, 2 t, 2 dg, 1 lg and 1 m x 2, 3 m, 2 dg, 3 t, 2 dg, 2 n, 2 t, 1 dg, 1 n, 1 dg, 1 lg, 1 m, 2 dg, 2 n, 1 m and 1 n x 2, 1 m, 7 lg, 2 t, 1 lg, 1 t, 1 lg, 2 m, 2 lg, 2 t, 2 m, 1 dg and 1 lg x 2, 1 t and 1 dg x 2, 1 lg, 3 t, 3 dg, 7 n, 1 m, 1 lg, 1 m, 1 n, 1 m and 1 lg x 3, 2 lg, 1 n, 1 lg, 1 dg, 1 lg and 1 n x 3, 1 dg, 1 lg, 1 dg, 1 t, 1 lg, 3 dg, 1 lg and 1 dg x 5.

Warp length: 4-Harness Frame Loom: 2¾ yards (use extender rods). Floor Loom: 3½ yards.

Weft: ¼-pound *each* of lime green and turquoise 1 ply #5 tightly spun Swedish worsted wool yarn. Picks per inch: 12.

Weave pattern: Satin Weave (see graph 55-B below for threading, treadling, and tie-up).

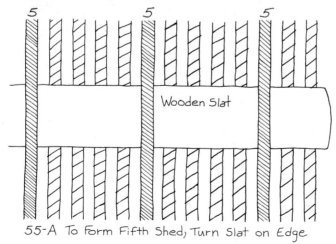

55-A To Form Fifth Shed, Turn Slat on Edge

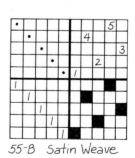

55-B Satin Weave

Finishing: Table runner—knotted fringe. Skirt—lining, seaming, waistband, and hemming.

HOW TO MAKE

1. Weave in a 2-inch heading, then begin to use lime green as the weft material and weave until 26½ inches have been completed. Keep the beat fairly light.
2. Change to turquoise weft and weave 15½ inches.
3. Return to the use of lime green for the weft and complete another 26½ inches.
4. Change back to turquoise weft and weave a final 15½ inches.

Finishing. Remove the fabric from the loom. Table Runner: Trim all fringe to about 6 inches and knot in pairs using an overhand knot as shown on page 25, photo 25-C. Press lightly with a steam iron to set the weave before using. Skirt: Consider the side of the fabric with the warp predominating as the face of the cloth. Fold the length of fabric in half across the length and mark the fold with pins. Next, lay the cloth out flat and sew *across* the length, ¼-inch on either side of the pin line. Cut between the two lines of stitches to separate the cloth into 2 panels. Also, sew across remaining 2 raw edges.

Cut two lengths of lining the same width and length as the skirt panels. Pin each lining to the wrong sides of each panel and baste. Pin both lined panels together, right sides facing, and sew down the edges until the beginning of the turquoise border along the bottom. As shown in drawing 56-A, baste under ¼-inch along the waist edge, then fold over ¾-inch to the inside of the skirt and, starting at a side seam, sew along the bottom edge of this fold to make a channel for the elastic. Leave about an inch unsewn to allow elastic to be inserted.

Cut the elastic to a size slightly larger than your waist measurement, pin a safety pin at one end and thread the elastic through the sewn channel. Sew the ends together and close the channel by hand (drawing 56-B).

To finish the side slits, turn the skirt inside out and iron all seams flat. Fold the lining under to fall between the lining and skirt *in line with* the sewn seam (drawing 56-C). Next, fold the woven fabric to the inside of the skirt, *overlapping* the folded edge of the lining (56-D). Pin and then sew by machine.

To hem, turn under ¼-inch of the woven fabric, then pin and sew it into place. Put on the skirt and measure the length of the hem by marking it with pins. Remove the skirt, turn it inside out, turn up the hem, and pin it securely. Hemstitch into place. Steam the skirt lightly to remove any creases or wrinkles.

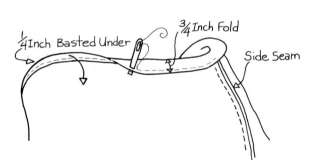

56-A Channel for Waist Elastic

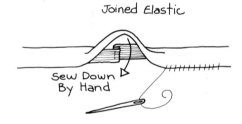

56-B Finishing Elastic Waistband

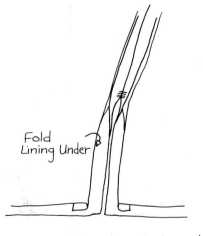

56-C Finishing Side Slits, A.

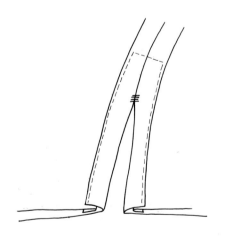

56-D Finishing Side Slits, B.

Twill Weave Shawl or Table Drape

(Color photo on page 59, top)

The subtle colorations of this hand-brushed woolen shawl or table drape result from pre-arranged color patterns in both the warp and the weft. Two simple twill patterns help to integrate colors; the needlewoven tassel fringe is reminiscent of a medieval garment trim.

Plaids and color changes. Color variations can be made by grouping one or more colors together in a particular sequence of stripes across the warp *or* across the weft. When these color groups are formed in *both* warp and weft, a plaid results. These sequences can be made from textural variations of a color or from a grouping of shades from one or more color families. The stripes might be wide or narrow, composed of one or many colors and textures or even arranged in the manner of gingham checks. Color and pattern variations are really endless.

This project is an excellent example of simple twill variations and the visual color blending so characteristic of weaving.

Equipment: 4-Harness Frame Loom: four stick shuttles, slat beater, scissors, tape measure, tapestry needle. Floor Loom: four stick shuttles, scissors, tape measure, tapestry needle.

Finished size: 19 inches by 60 inches, with fringe.

Warp: 1 pound cream-colored 3 ply woolen yarn, 3 ounces *each* of dark purple, lavender, and celery yellow 2 ply woolen yarn set 22 inches wide at 10 ends per inch. Warp Color Order from left to right: (7 yellow), (28 cream), (31 lavender), (1 cream followed by 1 lavender—repeat 42 times), (1 yellow followed by 1 lavender—repeat 5 times), (1 yellow followed by 1 cream—repeat 19 times), (15 white), and (7 purple).

Warp length: 4-Harness Frame Loom: 72 inches. Floor Loom: 2½ yards.

Weft: Same colors in same amounts as given for warp. Wind each color onto a separate shuttle and use as directed. Picks per inch: 2 ply-16; 3 ply-10.

Weaving pattern: Balanced twill, three and one twill, and plain weave (see graphs below for threading, treadling and tie up).

Finishing: Twining and needlewoven fringe; hand brushed surface.

HOW TO MAKE

1. Weave 9 inches of heading for fringe, then twine warp ends into place (drawing 57-A).

2. Weave 4 inches of tabby, using the cream-colored yarn.

3. The next inch is woven using the 3 and 1 twill (harness groups 123, 234, 341, 412 in that order), having 4 picks yellow, 4 picks deep purple, 2 picks yellow, 2 picks deep purple, 1 pick cream, 1 pick yellow, 1 pick deep purple, 1 pick cream, and 1 pick yellow.

4. Twelve inches are next woven in balanced twill (har-

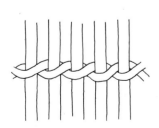

57-A Twining

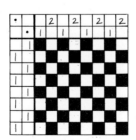

Plain Weave Graph

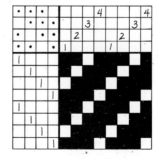

Three & One Twill Graph

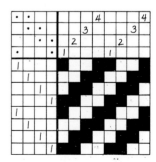

Balanced Twill Graph

ness groups 12, 23, 34, 41 in that order), using cream-colored yarn.

5. Make a 1/2-inch weft stripe of deep purple in the 3 and 1 twill.

6. The next two inches of yellow are made in the 3 and 1 twill.

7. Use lavender in the balanced twill for the next 4 inches.

8. Weave 2 inches of deep purple in the 3 and 1 twill.

9. Using the 3 and 1 twill, make the next 1 inch in celery yellow.

10. The next 12 inches are done in balanced twill, using the cream-colored yarn.

11. Three and one twill is used for the next 1 inch, having 1 pick yellow, 1 pick cream, 1 pick deep purple, 1 pick yellow, 1 pick cream, 1 pick deep purple, 1 pick yellow, 4 picks deep purple, 4 picks yellow, and 1 pick using 2 strands of yellow yarn at once.

12. Make the next 4 inches in tabby weave, using cream-colored yarn.

Finishing: Twine warp ends as at the beginning of the piece and then, leaving 9 inches for fringe at each end, cut the project from the loom.

To make the woven tassels with fringe, divide the loose fringe into 15 even groups of 12 ends each for 3 ply warp and 18 ends each for 2 ply warp. Each woven area has 6 vertical ribs, made by grouping the yarns 2 to a rib for 3 ply, and 3 to a rib for 2 ply and mixed ply tassel groups.

Using a blunt-tipped tapestry needle threaded with celery yellow, start next to the twining and, using the plain weave, make the first row (drawing 58-A). Tuck in the tail and continue to weave for 3/4-inch (a table fork can be used to beat the weft into place). At that point, weave only the two outside ribs for 1/2-inch (drawing 58-B). This will leave a "window" in the center of the tassel, adding visual interest. Return to weaving across the entire group of ends as at the beginning of the tassel for 1/2-inch.

Now make three ribs across the tassel by going over and under two groups of warp at once (drawing 58-C). This will slightly narrow the tassel. After 1/4-inch has been woven, divide the warp into only two groups for 1/4-inch, then unite into one group, wrapping 4 or 5 times. Run the yarn back up inside the tassel and clip it off (drawing 58-D). This gradual reduction of rib groups will put a natural curved and wrapped end to the tassel.

Trim the tassel's fringe to about 5 inches. Repeat across the warp to complete the trim. (The last tassel will have 7 ribs due to an uneven number of warp ends.)

Wash and block this shawl or table drape as you would a wool sweater, and then pin it down by the edges before it dries to prevent excessive shrinkage. When it has dried, brush all but the wide vertical center stripe with a firm bristle brush to bring up the nap.

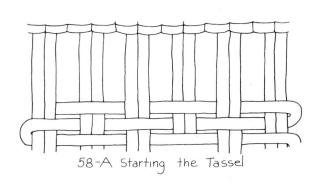

58-A Starting the Tassel

58-B Weaving the "Window"

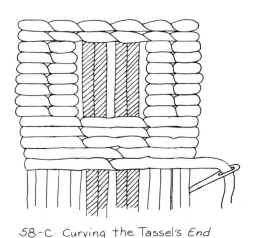

58-C Curving the Tassel's End

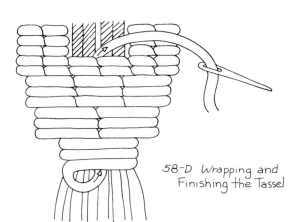

58-D Wrapping and Finishing the Tassel

WOVEN TASSELS trim this softly colored twill weave shawl **(at left);** brushed wool gives its surface a frosted appearance. Directions begin on page 57. The basket form shown in the two photos **(below)** can be hung as a sculptural wall decoration or suspended from overhead as a basket or plant container. Jute is used in the construction of this piece, which is explained on pages 60 and 61.

DESIGN: KLAUDIA HERROLD

DESIGN: GYONGY LAKY

Off-Loom Basket or Wall Hanging

(Color photos on page 59, bottom left and right)

Is it a basket . . . or a sculptural wall hanging? Well, it could be both. Designed for dual duty, this jute-rope woven basket-hanging is deceptively simple in concept. Plain weave, twining, loops, and diagonal weaving combine to shape this decorative yet useful piece.

Weaving a basket. Why has a basket been included in a book about weaving? Because basketmaking was probably one of the earliest forms of weaving practiced and has been a part of all cultures for a long time. Baskets are really only a three-dimensional adaptation of the techniques used to create a container. In this case it's weaving; in others, it might be knotless netting or macrame; however it's done, you'll need to think in more terms than merely *width* and *length*.

In a woven basket the addition of the third dimension of *height* is accomplished by manipulating the shape of the warp by weft yarns or grasses that are tightened, loosened, or redirected in their weaving path. Once these techniques have been mastered,

you're ready to try them out on grasses, reeds, weeds, green twigs, rope, or anything else that seems to lend itself to sculptural effects. The diversity of available raw materials will provide an opportunity for you to make exciting dimensional and textural discoveries.

The following project will start you on your way by demonstrating three basic methods of increasing and decreasing size for the control of shapes. The use of jute rope in the weaving provides bulk and texture; if your concept is more delicate, try heavy twine and rope materials or firm yarns with body.

Equipment: 12-inch by 12-inch square piece of heavy fiberboard, T-pins, scissors, tape measure.

Finished size: Approximately 14 inches by 16 inches by 6 inches, not including fringe.
Warp and weft: Cut 4- to 5-foot lengths of jute rope in the following amounts and colors—8 silver blue, 8 turquoise green, 10 magenta, 12 burnt orange, and

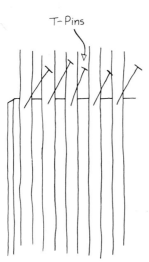

60-A Attaching Warp to Working Surface

60-B Twining the Pulled-Up Jute Loops

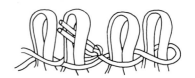

60-C How to Secure Ends of Twining

6 deep purple. If the jute is available only in natural tones, these colors can be easily achieved with household dyes. Purchase 1 package of red raffia and 1 small ball of sisal twine for finishing.

Finishing: Twining and uneven loose fringe.

HOW TO MAKE

1. Lay 14 lengths of jute out over the fiberboard square in this color order: 4 maroon, 4 purple, and 6 orange. Center them until there is an even amount of fringe above and below the edges of the board.

2. With the T-pins, tack each warp length securely along one edge of the board (drawing 60-A).

3. When the warp is secured, begin to weave in the remaining separate lengths of jute, using plain weave and following this color order: 6 turquoise green, 6 blue, and 2 maroon. Leave an equal amount of fringe on either side of the woven area and pack the weft as tightly as possible, using more T-pins to keep the weft in place. This is essential for giving body and form to the basket.

4. Now you should have a flat square of woven jute rope 14 strands by 14 strands. Remove the T-pins, cut a 3 to 4 yard length of red raffia, fold it in half, and begin to twine it around this square. The twining occurs around consecutive loops of jute that have been pulled up just at the edge of the woven square (drawing 60-B). When you have finished the twining, knot the remaining end of raffia and tuck it into the next jute loop (drawing 60-C).

5. The second level of the basket wall is formed by adding 4 more lengths of jute rope to each of the loop-twined edges of the original square. The color order is as follows—top: 4 lengths of burnt orange; right: 2 lengths of burnt orange, 2 of purple; bottom: 4 lengths of maroon; and left: 2 lengths of turquoise green, 2 of blue. Weave in these added lengths, and pack them tightly against the twined loops (drawing 61-A).

6. Pull up and twine loops around this second area of weaving just as was done to the edges of the original square. These rows of loops will remain on the outside of the basket, adding textural interest and dimension to the exterior decoration.

7. The exact *center* of each side in this final large square will mark the corners of the basket. Divide the jute lengths of each side exactly in half. This should give two groups of 7 lengths each for each side of the square.

8. Begin weaving *diagonally*, using the left hand group of 7 as warp and the right hand group of 7 as weft. This re-directs the shape of the basket by dividing in half the number of ends used for the warp and the weft. Drawing 61-B explains diagonal weaving.

9. As the sides of the basket move up, the second edge of twined loops will angle diagonally up and down the sides of the basket.

Finishing: When the diagonal weaving reaches a point 2 or 3 rows beyond the four uppermost corners of the twined loop trim (drawing 61-C), finish off the top edge of the basket opening with 3 or 4 rows of sisal twining pushed up tightly against the edge of the last woven area. Leave the fringe hanging at different lengths. The project may now be turned over and pushed into a container-like shape for use as a basket, or the outer side can be manipulated into a variety of shapes and hung by one corner from a wall hook.

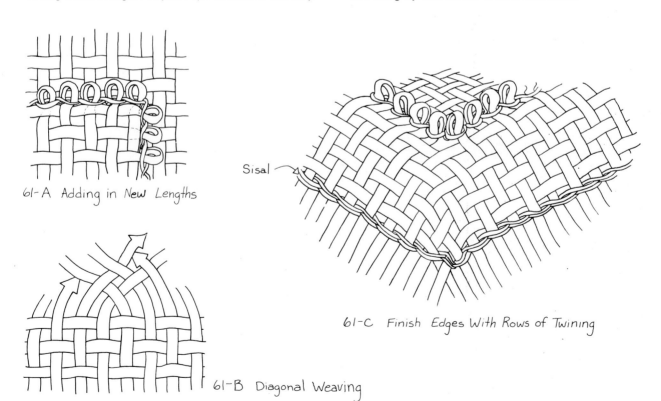

61-A Adding in New Lengths

Sisal

61-C Finish Edges With Rows of Twining

61-B Diagonal Weaving

DESIGN: MARI SPEYER AND K. LEE MANUEL

NEEDLEWOVEN DOLL *(at left)* is really a plump pillow. Directions begin on facing page. Indian double ikat is shown in the two photos at **lower left.** Both warp and weft are intricately tied and dyed many times, coloring the individual threads in a manner that produces a finished pattern in the fabric if both are properly aligned when woven together *(upper photo).* This process produces a cloth patterned with delicate color areas *(lower photo).* Baule wrap-around cloth *(lower right)* comes from the Ivory Coast. Partial indigo ikat and varicolored silk brocade work decorate the cotton ground of this Tiebissou man's toga.

COURTESY GYONGY LAKY

LOWIE MUSEUM OF ANTHROPOLOGY, UNIVERSITY OF CALIFORNIA, BERKELEY

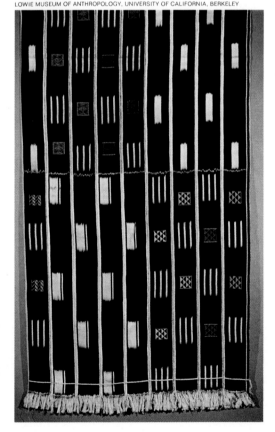

Painted Warp Doll

(Color photo on facing page, top)

Here is a perky pillow doll that will welcome your child with open arms. Needlewoven on a shaped cardboard loom, the doll is done in pastel yarn tones over a hand-painted warp in corresponding colors.

Painted warp. This is a variation based on ikat, or tie-dyed warp, for which portions of the warp are tightly wrapped before dyeing. When the wrapping is removed after dyeing, the undyed areas form a distinct pattern. For painted warp, textile paints are used to transfer a design onto closely set warp yarn, which is then woven. This makes a painted warp-faced cloth. In another version, the warp is more widely spaced; a colored cartoon is placed under the warp as a guide for painting on the design (if a small or shaped piece is desired, the cartoon can be drawn directly onto a notched cardboard loom). The warp is wound onto the loom, painted to correspond to the cartoon, and woven, using correspondingly colored yarns for each painted area. This is the technique used for the pillow doll.

Equipment: Shaped cardboard loom, red, yellow, white, and blue textile paints (mix to get intermediate colors), tapestry needle, scissors, ruler, small oil paint brush, polyester batting, and a medium crochet hook.

Finished size: about 15 inches by 18 inches.
Warp: 1 ounce (120 yards) 4 ply white cotton carpet warp set at 8 ends to the inch across the cardboard loom. Wind the warp *around* the loom from top to bottom, front to back. It should completely *encase* the body of the loom.

Weft: 1½ ounces *each* pink, yellow, red, orange, green, mauve, and turquoise one-ply Mexican hand-spun wool. Number of picks per inch varies from 10 to 12.
Weaving pattern: Plain weave (drawing 63-A).
Finishing: Stuffing, handsewing, and reinforcing.

HOW TO MAKE

1. Enlarge the loom design on page 64 to the correct size and transfer it to heavy cardboard. Cut out two loom shapes, one with the cardboard ribs running across the loom and one with the ribs running vertically. Glue them together to make a strong loom, drying overnight before using.
2. With a ruler, mark vertical lines (8 per inch) lengthwise across the loom. This will be a guide for cutting ¼-inch deep notches and for winding on the warp.
3. Warp the loom, keeping the yarn fairly loose; as it is woven, the tension will increase. Following the design drawn on the loom, paint the warp front and back with undiluted textile paint. Allow to dry overnight.
4. Starting at the top of the loom, thread a tapestry needle with an 18-inch length of yarn in the indicated color and begin to work in plain weave, using the tip of the needle or a small comb to beat the weft into place. Don't beat too tightly; the warp should show. (For information on needle weaving, see pages 20 and 21.)
5. As you weave, go *around* the doll, making a continuous path from front to back to front to create a

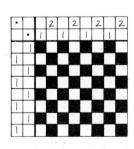

63-A Plain Weave

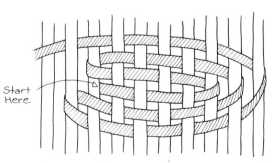

63-B Weaving Lozenge Areas

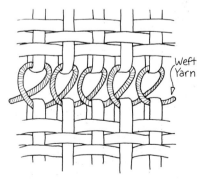

63-C Closing Lower Edges

pillow form which is closed on all three sides.

6. When joining color areas, be sure to dovetail joins or make diagonal slits (see page 45 drawings B and C). This will prevent vertical slit openings that will have to be sewn shut later. Lozenge-shaped areas (eyes, mouth, flowers, and so forth) are woven as shown in drawing 63-B.

7. Leave one inch of warp unwoven along bottom edge for selvage. Cut carefully along the bottom edge and lift woven cloth off loom from bottom to top.

Finishing: Machine zig-zag or whipstitch unfinished edge by hand to prevent unravelling; then stuff the doll, turn in selvages, and sew closed by hand (see drawing 63-C). Reinforce along all edges by needle-weaving weft yarn in the correct colors as required .

Each Square Equals 1 Inch

Warp Face Belt or Bell Pull

(Color photos on page 66, top left and right)

Long enough for a sash, wide enough for a bell pull —this warp-face fringed weaving can take on either personality. Carpet yarns in blueberry and autumn colors form the weaving's thick, rug-like texture.

Warp face rep. The basic plain weave can be varied by introducing a technique known as *rep*. For warp-face, this means setting the warp so densely together that no weft yarn shows except at the selvages. (Weft-face rep is also possible; good example is rib weave.)

Color changes in warp face rep are made by alternately warping two shades of color for each individual row of color blocks moving *down* the face of the cloth. One color is threaded onto the first harness, the second color to the second harness. When harness one is raised, the first color rides on the surface; when harness two rises, the second color comes to the surface, forming a contrasting block (see drawings 65-A and 65-B, below).

If a vertical row of plain color is desired, the same colored yarn warped sequentially is threaded on to adjacent harnesses. Many other geometric patterns can be made as is shown in the sample drafts below (drawing 65-C). The top row in each draft is the second harness and the bottom row is the first; dark squares are color 1, and x-marked squares are color 2.

Equipment: 4-Harness Frame Loom (use only two of the harnesses): small stick shuttle, scissors, tape measure. Floor Loom: small stick shuttle, scissors, tape measure.

Finished size: 2½ inches by 64 inches.
Warp: 1 ounce *each* of maroon, violet, purple, and dusty pink; 1½ ounces of rust; and 2 ounces of burnt orange 3-ply wool carpet yarn set 2½ inches wide at 21 ends to the inch.
Warp color order: See drawing 65-D below.
Warp length: 4-Harness Frame Loom: 2 yards. Floor Loom: 3 yards.
Weft: 1 ounce burnt orange 3-ply wool carpet yarn. Picks per inch: 3½.
Weave pattern: Plain weave (see page 63 for graph).
Finishing: Belt: fringe and weft locking tie; Bell Pull: Swiss cow bell and wall hook added by sewing.

HOW TO MAKE

1. Start first weft pass about 10 inches up from bottom of warp, leaving a 10-inch weft tail hanging loose. This will later become a part of the fringe.
2. Change sheds and make second pass, pulling weft very tight to draw warp ends together. Change shed again, beat previous row into place with side of stick shuttle, and then pass the weft again. Keep weft tight to avoid loops at the selvages.
3. Continue until 44 inches have been woven. Leaving a 10-inch weft tail, cut weft, then cut all warp ends 10 inches from last weft pass to make fringe.

Finishing: Remove piece from loom, tying each 10-inch weft tail with a square knot to the last warp end of fringe opposite the side where the tail emerges. To make a bell pull, attach a cow bell 4 inches up from the bottom. Fold over at 18 inches up from this end and attach a wall hook or dowel at that point for hanging.

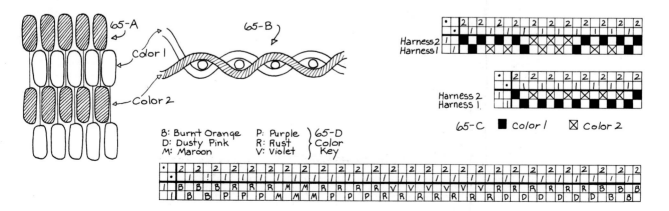

B: Burnt Orange P: Purple
D: Dusty Pink R: Rust 65-D Color Key
M: Maroon V: Violet

65-C ■ Color 1 ☒ Color 2

WARP FACED BELT **(below)** *can be transformed into a colorful bell-pull* **(at left)** *by addition of Swiss cow bell. Directions on page 65.*

DESIGN: PHYLLIS BIGELOW

COURTESY PHYLLIS BIGELOW

INTRICATE PICK-UP PATTERN of this handwoven belt from Guatemala **(lower right)** *is formed by two sets of complementary colored threads finger manipulated to form color reverse patterns on either side of the woven strip. Belts such as this one are woven on looms similar to the Guatemalan backstrap loom shown* **below.**

Reed and Grass Table Mat

(Color photo on page 68, top)

Maximum good looks with a minimum of expenditure —that's our placemat *au naturel*. Found bark, grasses, bamboo, and purchased raffia are combined in a simple plain weave, every ingredient direct from nature, unprocessed and pure.

Using materials directly from nature. Most bark, grasses, weeds, leaves, branches, or even roots can be dried and used for weaving with no further treatment. The materials used in this placemat were gathered from vacant lots, wooded areas, and a bamboo grove near the artist's home. Drying was quickly accomplished by placing the materials in the trunk of a car and leaving them there for two or three warm days. The dry heat from the running car removed moisture without fading any natural coloring. You may not find bamboo in your locale, but you could certainly substitute other native plant materials.

Equipment: Stretcher bar frame loom 18 inches by 24 inches with 4 nails to the inch, bodkin or large, blunt tapestry needle, comb beater, pick-up stick, scissors, tape measure.

Finished size: 15 inches by 21 inches.
Warp: 1 package of raffia set 13 inches wide at 8 ends to the inch.
Warp length: 24 inches (to warp nail loom, see drawing 67-A, below). Knot new raffia in at nails.
Weft: four 15 inch lengths of bamboo, five 15 inch strips of brown bark, one pound dried grasses at least 15 inches long, and remaining raffia from warp.
Weaving pattern: Plain weave using needleweaving approach and pick-up stick to form the sheds.
Finishing: twining and knotted fringe.

HOW TO MAKE

1. Space out warp by twining with single raffia strand.
2. Weave three rows of tabby, using tapestry needle threaded with a single strand of raffia.
3. Open the next two sheds by using the pick-up stick to separate alternating warp ends (drawing 67-B). Fill each shed with bamboo, then remove pick-up stick.
4. Weave four rows of tabby in single strand raffia; for the next three sheds, use pick-up stick to open sheds and bunch about ten strands of raffia for each individual weft pass.
5. Next, weave two single raffia picks followed by a strip of bark. Repeat. Follow with two picks single raffia tabby and two picks bunched grasses as in the last part of step 4.
6. Pass three rows single raffia tabby, one row bunched raffia, one row single raffia tabby, one row bunched grasses, and one row bunched raffia.
7. Make one row single raffia tabby, one row bark strip, one pick bunched raffia, two rows single raffia tabby, and one row bark strip.
8. Follow with one row small bunched grasses (eight strands per bunch), one pick thin bark strip, four rows single raffia tabby, two rows bunched raffia, and one pick large strip of bark.
9. Next, weave two rows double raffia tabby, three picks bunched raffia, three rows single raffia tabby, and two rows bamboo.

Finishing: Make seven rows of single raffia tabby and twine all warp ends as at beginning of mat. Remove from loom, knot off all warp ends, and trim fringes with a pair of sharp scissors.

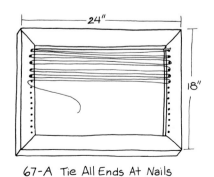

67-A Tie All Ends At Nails

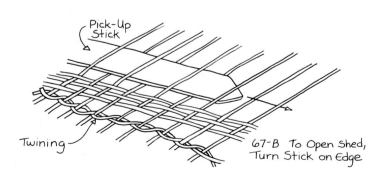

Pick-Up Stick

Twining

67-B To Open Shed, Turn Stick on Edge

DESIGN: LAURA FOLGER

A NATURAL FIBER table mat that shows off ceramic tableware to perfection was constructed from dried grasses, bamboo, raffia, and bark strips. Directions begin on page 67.

LOWIE MUSEUM OF ANTHROPOLOGY, UNIVERSITY OF CALIFORNIA, BERKELEY

TLINGIT INDIAN blanket (above), dating from 1910, was found near Skagway, Alaska. Woven on a warp composed of yellow cedar bark plied with handspun mountain goat wool, this shaped ceremonial blanket was colored with natural dyes including hemlock bark and lichens. Plain and twill twining, inlay, and plaiting were used in its construction. "Autumn" (right) lives up to its name, using colors and materials that bring this season to mind. Natural slub silk makes up the exposed warp; dried palm branches and natural handspun wool construct the weft decoration.

DESIGN: SYLVIA LOVELL-COOPER

*THREE-DIMENSIONAL weaving often takes the form of baskets. Weaves used in these baskets are **(clockwise from left)** plain weave, twill weave, twining, rep weave.*

DESIGN: MARI SPEYER

BIRCH BARK strips and fine yarns in autumn leaf colors weave a papery wall hanging. Hung on its side, this decorative piece was originally woven from left to right. The fringe was added by hand later.

Gingham Rag Pillow

(Color photo on facing page, top)

Yarns aren't the only raw materials for a weaving, as is evidenced by the use of rag strips in the construction of this pillow. The gingham checks result from alternating blue and white stripes in both warp and weft.

Gingham checks. This design is formed not from a complicated weaving pattern but from color groupings in the warp and weft. Gingham usually consists of groups of white alternating with groups of another color in the warp and in the weft, plus a third color formed at the points where they meet and cross one another. Knowing how gingham is constructed will enable you to recognize it and other woven color patterns in the fabrics around you.

Equipment: Simple frame loom measuring 40 inches by 20 inches (see page 10 for directions), pick-up stick, two stick shuttles, scissors, tape measure, sewing needle, white and blue thread, size K crochet hook, polyester batting.

Finished size: 15 inches by 28 inches.
Warp: 1½ yards *each* of plain blue cotton cloth and plain white cotton cloth 36 inches wide in a plain weave. Each length is cut into 1-inch-wide strips that are sewn together end to end to form two continuous lengths of cloth strip, one in blue and one in white. Set the warp 18 inches wide at 5 ends to the inch.
Warp color order: 12 ends of blue followed by 12 ends of white—repeat this order 4 times.
Warp length: 40 inches.
Weft: Follow same amounts, colors, and procedure given for warp but wind each continuous color strip onto 2 separate shuttles. Picks per inch: 4.

Weaving pattern: Plain Weave (weave as directed below. There is no threading, treadling, or tie-up).
Finishing: Fringe and side lacing; stuffing.

HOW TO MAKE

1. Twine warp ends into place six inches up from the bottom nails with a rag strip.
2. For plain weave shed, use pick-up stick as shown in drawing 70-A. Turn stick on edge, pass blue strip (leave 2 inch tail), turn stick flat, and beat weft into place. Remove stick. Form alternate shed with shed stick, pass second pick of blue, tuck in 2 inch tail of rag strip, and beat into place.
3. Continue this order until 9 picks of blue have been woven, then cut the blue strip 1 inch beyond the selvage and sew it to the free end of the continuous white rag strip (drawing 70-B). (Be sure to form squares across the face of the pillow; if 9 picks aren't enough, add more until a square is formed.)
4. Make next 9 picks of white, sewing the end of the white strip to the blue strip as in step 3.
5. Continue to alternate 9 picks of blue with 9 picks of white until 12 weft stripes have been woven, 6 stripes of blue alternating with 6 stripes of white.
6. To remove pillow from loom, cut warp end loops open, tying them loosely to prevent unraveling.

Finishing. Join sides as shown in drawing 70-C, using 2 yard strips of cloth for edges. Stuff the pillow and close the bottom edge as shown in drawing 70-D.

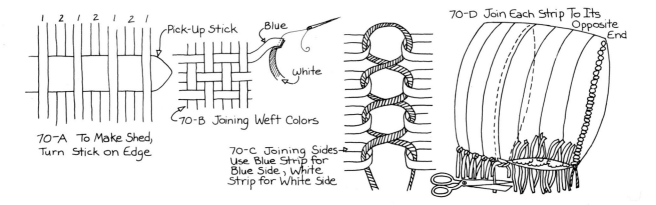

70-A To Make Shed, Turn Stick on Edge

70-B Joining Weft Colors

70-C Joining Sides—Use Blue Strip for Blue Side, White Strip for White Side

70-D Join Each Strip To Its Opposite End

DESIGN: KATHRYN HERRMAN

GINGHAM CHECK pillow **(left)** uses rag strips for rows of color in warp and weft, which intersect to form a two-tone check pattern. Examples of Ashanti kente cloth are shown at the **lower left.** Kente, a prestige cloth of the Ashanti and related groups, exhibits brocade and overweave patterns having many particular names and symbolic meanings. "Senkeni," **(at left)** is a traditional kente pattern; "Mmaeda", **(at right),** is considered unique. Both pieces—made of unraveled trade silk—were collected in Ghana. Quilted rag strip pillow **(lower right)** has cotton warp woven in a plain weave.

LOWIE MUSEUM OF ANTHROPOLOGY, UNIVERSITY OF CALIFORNIA, BERKELEY

DESIGN: MARI SPEYER

Leno Lace Shirt

(Color photo on page 74, top)

Subtle texture and design give character to this plum-colored plain weave linen shirt. Sleeves, hem, and neckline are delicately accentuated by leno lace weave, lending a soft, feminine touch to the garment.

Leno lace technique. Before a leno area is begun, a few rows of tabby should be woven. Pause when a shed is opened that raises the right-hand outside warp end of the area to be leno'ed. Temporarily set aside the weft filling for a pointed pick-up stick and, starting at the right-hand edge of the area to be leno'ed, lift the first warp end in the *lower shed* to the right of, up, and over the first warp end in the upper shed with the pointed tip of the pick-up stick. This causes a twist in these two warp ends. Now pick up the next warp end in the lower shed and bring it to the right of, up, and over the next warp end in the upper shed (drawing 72-A). Continue this movement from right to left across the entire area to be leno'ed.

Close the shed, turn the stick on its edge, and pass the weft filling through this leno shed, then remove the pick-up stick. Beat carefully after stick is removed to place leno evenly across the warp. Don't beat too firmly—the appearance of leno is open and lace-like.

The next weft shot should be in the plain weave shed, causing the twisted warp ends to untwist. Leno may be used to good advantage in such projects as table furnishings, curtains or garment trims. Methods used for making leno lace are shown in drawings 72-B and 72-C.

Equipment: 4-Harness Frame Loom: three stick or boat shuttles, slat beater and comb beater, pick-up stick, scissors, tape measure, tapestry needle. Floor Loom: three boat shuttles, pick-up stick, scissors, tape measure, tapestry needle.

Finished size: Body—18½ inches by 50 inches; Sleeves—18½ inches by 19 inches each. This is a medium size; for other sizes measure hips, length from neck to hem, and length from shoulder to wrist, then make a muslin shirt to these measurements to get the proper sizing. Yarn amounts will vary with size.

Warp: 8 ounces *each* of purple, rose, and deep blue 20/2 linen set 21 inches wide at 18 ends to the inch.

Warp color order: Purple, rose, deep blue sequence repeated across entire warp. All three colors can be wound at the same time to speed warping.

Warp length: 4-Harness Frame Loom: 112 inches (add

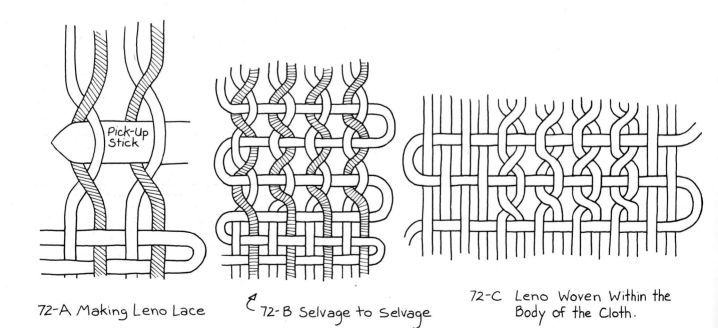

72-A Making Leno Lace   72-B Selvage to Selvage   72-C Leno Woven Within the Body of the Cloth.

25-inch extender rods); Floor Loom: 11 feet.

Weft: 8 ounces *each* of purple, rose, and deep blue 20/2 linen. Wind each color onto a separate shuttle and use as directed. Picks per inch: 18.

Weaving pattern: Plain weave (see graph on page 75 for threading, treadling, and tie-up) and leno lace.

Finishing: 6-plied fringe, cross-stitched seams, and re-woven warp threads at neck opening.

HOW TO MAKE

Refer to drawing 73-A for garment measurements.

1. Body: Weave 2 inches of heading to allow for fringe, then 6 picks of plain weave using three shuttles (each wound with one color) and following the purple, rose, deep blue color repeat used in the warp. For directions on using more than one shuttle, see page 23.
2. Weave 2¼ inches selvage to selvage leno lace, passing all three colors simultaneously in the leno sheds. Separate each row of leno with 3 rows of plain weave in the purple, rose, deep blue order, using each color singly.
3. Weave 15 inches of plain weave, repeating the purple, rose, deep blue color order in the weft.
4. Make a full size heavy paper pattern of the entire leno neck design (drawing 73-B) and use it as a pattern or guide for placing leno lace. Weave a 4-inch slit, using tapestry slit technique (see pages 44 and 45 for detailed instructions), and make tabby-separated leno rows along the slit, following the outline of the paper pattern (drawing 73-C). Use purple, rose, deep blue repeat simultaneously in the leno lace sheds within the lace areas but return to individual use of purple, rose, and deep blue in the plain weave sheds.
5. When semicircular neck opening is reached, con-

tinue to follow the neck design pattern outline for 5 inches, using the same leno and plain weave weft order as outlined in step 4. As you go, fill in the warp threads falling within the neck opening itself with some kind of filler to keep tension constant across the warp. This will be removed when the neck area is finished.
6. At the finish of the semicircular neck opening, return to passing the weft from selvage to selvage, working in a 4-inch-deep half circle of leno lace at the back of the neck following the outline of the pattern.
7. Weave 20 inches of plain weave, then finish off the shirt body with 2¼ inches of leno lace and plain weave from selvage to selvage as at beginning of the shirt.
8. Fill in 4 inches of warp after the shirt body to allow for fringe, then begin the first sleeve.
9. Sleeves: Weave 8 inches of leno lace and plain weave as worked on hem of shirt, followed by 12 inches of plain weave. Leave 4 inches between sleeves for fringe, filling in this area with a heavy yarn to keep correct warp tension. Then make a second sleeve in the same way.
10. Remove pieces from loom and cut apart between sleeves and shirt back, removing headings and spacers. Leave 2 inches of fringe on the ends of each piece.

Finishing. Encase plain weave end of sleeves in 2-fold bias tape, sewing tape into place to prevent unraveling. To finish neck opening, remove filler and cut across warp threads at the center, none shorter than ½ inch. Use tapestry needle to weave two ends at a time back into the cloth (see page 25 for directions).

Fringe is 2-plied together, twisted in groups of three, and knotted at ends (see page 25 for directions). Center the sleeves at shoulders of shirt body and attach, cross-stitching by hand (drawing 73-D); place bias tape covered edge on the inside of the shirt. Join sleeve underarms and side seams of shirt with cross-stitch, leaving 4-inch slits at shirt hem. Wash shirt in warm water to shrink, then dry and press.

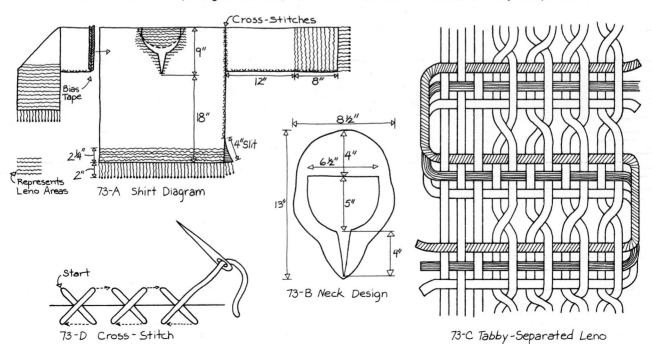

73-A Shirt Diagram

73-B Neck Design

73-D Cross-Stitch

73-C Tabby-Separated Leno

DESIGN: JANE MALEK

*LENO LACE accents the sleeves, neckline, and hem of this crushed-grape-colored summer shirt **(left)**. Directions begin on page 72. "Snow Cave" **(lower left)** has a cool airy feeling, enhanced by the use of white linen in a spaced warp and weft. Porcelain electrical insulators, looking very much like icicles, were used as accents. Peruvian handwork **(below)** dates from approximately 1500 A.D. From the Late Horizon period, this fragment of brown cotton gauze is decorated with polychrome bird designs in alpaca wool tapestry.*

LOWIE MUSEUM OF ANTHROPOLOGY, UNIVERSITY OF CALIFORNIA, BERKELEY

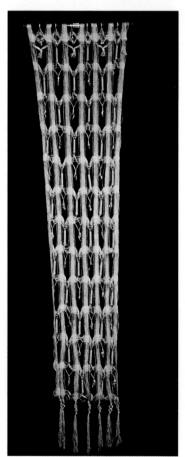

DESIGN: CHARLES M. ROSS

Inlaid Tunic or Shawl

(Color photos on page 76, top left and right)

A wrap for all reasons (and seasons), this plain weave tunic or shawl is enhanced by the addition of inlay diamonds and undulating borders. The decoration is simply laid in with the weft as weaving progresses. The optional tapestry-slit tunic-neck opening is also worked as the article is woven.

Inlay technique. Wind one butterfly bobbin of the inlay pattern color for each area to be laid-in (to stand out properly, the pattern color should contrast sufficiently with the background color). Decide on graph paper or by measurement where the patterns are to be laid in, then weave up to that point. Open the next shed and pass the background weft from selvage to selvage, beating it into place. Leaving the shed open, begin the butterfly by tucking a two inch tail through to the back of the shed at the point where the pattern begins. Insert the butterfly into the shed opening, move from one side of the inlay design to the other, close the shed, and beat. Open the next shed, pass background color, beat, and then make second pass of inlay color and beat into place.

When a weft pass is completed, either leave the butterfly on the face of the weaving or drop it through to the back until the next laid-in pass is made. If the butterfly remains on the face of the weaving, the turning loop will be on the surface; if it falls to the back, the turning loop will be on the back of the weaving (see drawings 75-A and 75-B, below). Continue until the inlay pattern is complete.

Equipment: 4-Harness Frame Loom: shuttle, slat beater, hand butterflies or tapestry needle, scissors, tape measure. Floor Loom: shuttle, hand butterflies or tapestry needle, scissors, tape measure.

Finished size: 20 inches by 62 inches.
Warp: 8 ounces red Scandinavian-type one-ply woolen yarn set 20½ inches wide at 12 ends to the inch with doubled warp ends at the selvages (put last two selvage threads on each side through the same heddle).
Warp length: 4-Harness Frame Loom: 85 inches (add 17-inch extender rods); Floor Loom: 3 yards.
Weft: 8 ounces each of red and maroon Scandinavian-type one-ply woolen yarn. Wind both colors onto one shuttle and use together for weft filling. Picks per inch: 7. Provide 4 ounces purple Scandinavian-type one-ply woolen yarn for laid-in designs.
Weaving pattern: plain weave (see graph below for threading, treadling, and tie-up).
Finishing: Twining and 4-plied fringe.

HOW TO MAKE

1. Warp the loom. Weave 10 inches of heading to allow for fringe, then twine the warp ends into place (for diagram see page 17). When using 4-harness frame loom, remember also to twine warp ends into place before weaving the heading.

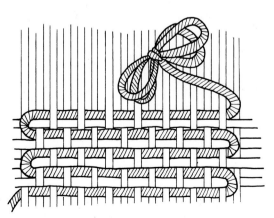

75-A   Surface Turn Loops

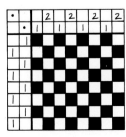

Plain Weave

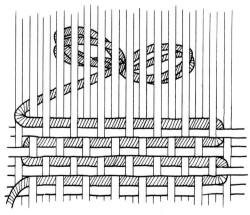

75-B   Hidden Turn Loops

DESIGN: MARILYN GELLER

*DIAMOND INLAID tunic **(above)** creates a dramatic costume; or leave out the tapestry slit neck opening, using the fringed fabric as a shawl **(above right).** Directions begin on page 75. Guatemalan backstrap loom produced this inlaid warp faced length of decorative cloth **(lower right).** Such lengths are often used as ornamental panels in many types of Guatemalan clothing.*

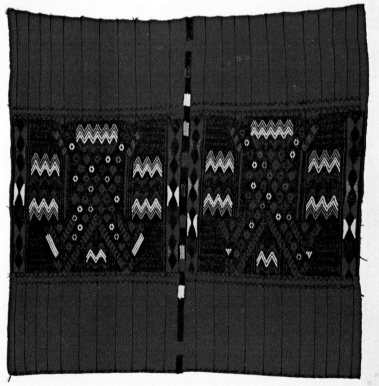

COURTESY PHYLLIS BIGELOW

DESIGN: ALYSON SMITH GONSALVES

DESIGN: MARI SPEYER

ENGLISH WORSTED yarns in sea colors form the body of the man's ruana, inlaid with silver grey fish (above). Rich Renaissance flavor is captured in a woolen dress (above right), worked in an advanced form of tapestry. A cartoon was used for color placement and shaping. *"Obi" (below left) is a pink cascade of tapestry, wrapping, cording, and feathers. Dramatic blue and white cape (below right) was shaped on the loom and woven in a twill variation threading.*

DESIGN: SACHI HONMYO

DESIGN: MARI SPEYER

2. Weave 3 inches, then begin inlay pattern. Start 2 inches in from the right selvage, cross to the opposite side and pull the butterfly to the surface 2 inches before reaching the left selvage.

3. Make the second weft pass with background color only and beat into place.

4. On the third pass, lay in the pattern yarn and return to the right selvage, stopping 2 inches short of the selvage edge with the butterfly on the surface.

5. Use this butterfly to make the right-hand border pattern, as shown in 78-A below, passing the inlay pattern color with every other weft shot. The first two inlay passes are 2 inches in length, the second two are 1¾ inches in length; both with loose turn loops on the surface.

6. Start a new butterfly for the left-hand border pattern at a point that is 2 picks directly above the first turn loop on the left hand side. Work the left and right borders simultaneously as you weave; they should line up across from one another. Continue this border the full length of the piece until arriving at a point 3 inches before the end of the piece. Then repeat the beginning portion of the inlay pattern to complete the border.

7. Five inches up from the twining and 8 inches in from both selvages, begin the two diamond shaped inlays (see drawing 78-B, below). The widest point of each diamond is 18 warp threads, 9 showing on the face of the pattern and 9 on the back. Turn loops are on the wrong side of the tunic or shawl.

8. When this is finished, weave 1½ inches more, then begin a large centered diamond whose width at the widest point is 40 warp threads, 20 on the surface and 20 on the wrong side.

9. Weave 2½ inches past the large diamond, then begin two more small diamonds of the same size and placement as the first pair of small diamonds. Repeat this pair 5 times at intervals of 3 inches to give 6 sets of diamonds, not counting the first pair.

10. If a neck opening is desired, begin the tapestry slit centered at 23½ inches from the bottom edge of the weaving. Use two shuttles for background color, one for each side of the 12-inch-long slit (for detailed instructions on weaving slits, see pages 44 and 45).

11. Two and one-half inches after the final pair of diamonds, lay in another large, centered diamond the same size as the first large, centered diamond.

12. When completed, weave 1½ inches more, then lay in the final pair of small diamonds, matching their size and placement to the very first pair of diamonds to be laid in.

13. Weave 3 inches, then complete the border design and weave for 3 inches more beyond the border. At this point, twine all warp ends into place.

Finishing. Remove the tunic or shawl from the loom, leaving 10 inches of warp at the end for fringe. Remove heading yarn. Ply fringe together by twisting two pair of warp ends to the right until taut. Then hold the two twisted pairs together and twist them around one another to the left (see drawing 78-C, below). If twisted tightly enough, the plied fringe won't unwind.

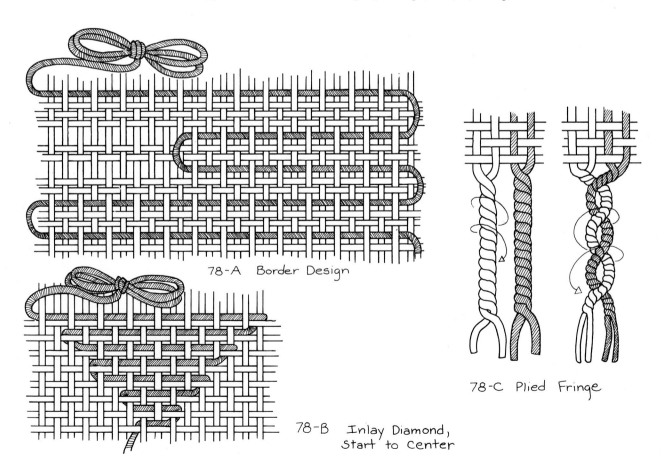

78-A Border Design

78-B Inlay Diamond, Start to Center

78-C Plied Fringe

LOWIE MUSEUM OF ANTHROPOLOGY, UNIVERSITY OF CALIFORNIA, BERKELEY

DESIGN: JO WILLRODT

*WEDGE-WOVEN Navajo blanket **(above)** has sloping designs in the weft built up with weft rows put in slantwise on a wedge of short weft rows. Huichol woolen yarns from Mexico weave dramatic tapestry and honeycomb patterned hanging **(above*

*right).** "Mali Mali" **(below left)** consists of three lashed branches covered with tapestry, rya, macrame, and wrapping. Red silk warp brocade is gradually added to white cotton twill ground in "On Target" **(below right).**

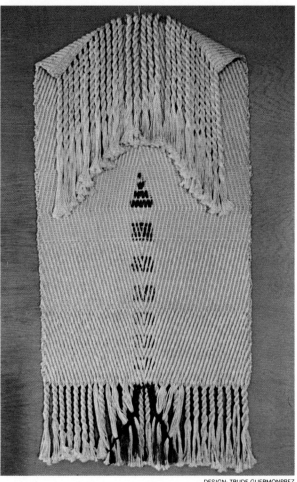

DESIGN: SYLVIA LOVELL-COOPER

DESIGN: TRUDE GUERMONPREZ

PROJECTS: PHOTOS **79**

Index

All projects are listed below in *italic* type.

Photographers

Ed Bigelow: 9 bottom, 66 lower left. **Fred R. Buskirk:** 46 lower left. **Lawrence Cuneo:** 79 lower right. **Alyson Smith Gonsalves:** 51 lower right. **Gyongy Laky:** 62 lower left top and bottom. **Roger M. Lovell-Cooper:** 43 lower left, 51 lower left, 68 lower right, 74 lower left, 79 lower left. **Ells Marugg:** 4, 5 all, 7, 8 all, 9 top, 10 all, 13 all, 14 all, 20 all, 21 all, 25 all, 26 all, 27 all, 28, 29, 33 all, 35 all, 38 all, 43 top, 46 lower right, 62 lower right, 66 lower right, 68 lower left, 69 top, 71 lower left, 74 lower right, 76 bottom, 79 upper left. **Lars Speyer:** 43 lower right, 46 top, 51 top, 54 all, 59 all, 62 top, 66 upper left and upper right, 68 top, 69 bottom, 71 top and lower right, 74 top, 76 upper left and upper right, 77 all, 79 upper right.